Designed to Con

The Blueprint of the Hidden Love Economy

Teo Lo Piparo

Dedication

"To my family —

To my wife, whose love steadies me.

To my son, whose wonder reminds me why.

And to all of you — parents, siblings, kin by blood or choice —

thank you for holding space for who I was, who I am,

and who I'm still becoming."

Prologue: Why This Book, Why Now

We are living in a time of paradox.

Global connection has never been easier, yet loneliness is at epidemic levels. Our tools are smarter, yet our systems feel increasingly fragile. Economic growth accelerates, yet trust, well-being, and belonging decline.

We don't suffer from a lack of intelligence. We suffer from a lack of integration. A failure to remember that love, not sentiment, but structure, is what makes anything worth building truly endure.

This book is for leaders, designers, entrepreneurs, educators, changemakers, and dreamers who sense that something essential has been lost, and are ready to build systems that honor the complexity, dignity, and beauty of being human.

It is not a manual in the traditional sense. It is a lens. A rhythm. A return.

It explores the types of love we must understand, not only to build strong relationships, but to create regenerative systems that don't just sustain life, but enrich it.

If you've ever wondered:

What does it mean to scale care without diluting it?

How can an economy be generous, and still resilient?

What would it look like to lead a company or team from clarity, not coercion?

...then you are holding the right book.

You will not find simple answers here. You will find language for what your intuition already knows, and design ideas for what your heart already dares to imagine.

Because it's not enough to feel love. We must design with it.

Table of Contents

Ignition Love: The Spark of Evolution

Before we could name it, we needed it. Love was not a feeling, but a function: the first flicker in the dark, the spark that urged us to reach, to call out, to survive. Before language, there was longing. And before longing, there was need.

Just as love began as function before feeling, markets arose from necessity before theory. The Silk Road wasn't created by economists theorizing about comparative advantage; it emerged because communities needed what others had. The spice trade, the search for salt, the quest for clean water, these weren't luxuries but survival imperatives that shaped entire civilizations.

When we attempt to give form to thought, we step into the fog of abstraction. An idea is rarely born ready. It trembles, unfinished, inside its carrier, shaped by lenses no one else wears. And yet, it must be shared. It is the only beginning we know: to move from the ineffable toward the intimate, to speak the unspeakable, even if imperfectly.

Shakespeare once wrote, "We are such stuff as dreams are made on, and our little life is rounded with sleep." These are the words of Prospero, exiled Duke and conjurer, who sees in the briefness of life a mirror of dreams. Fleeting, fragile, and yet filled with meaning. Sleep, in this context, is more than rest. It is the soft veil between one story and the next, the rhythm by which we measure all that matters.

A dream is not escape, it is rehearsal. A simulation of alternate futures, in which love survives, in which the self-expands. Evolution did not give us dreams to entertain us, it gave us dreams to help us adapt.

When Florence Nightingale reimagined hospitals not as places of passive suffering but as engines of recovery through hygiene, light, and data, she wasn't escaping war, she was rehearsing a future public health system that didn't yet exist.

When the Quakers in 18th-century England dreamed of commerce without exploitation, they rehearsed an economy of conscience. Their experiments with fair labor, anti-slavery supply chains, and ethical banking laid foundations for modern social enterprise long before those terms existed.

Take the early cooperative movement in 19th-century Rochdale: a group of working-class weavers envisioned a store owned by its members, practicing transparency, shared profit, and democratic control. Their dream wasn't utopian, it was a rehearsal for what later became the global co-op movement.

Even further back, when medieval Islamic scholars introduced waqf (charitable endowments), they weren't just funding mosques and schools, they were rehearsing economic systems that redirected wealth into long-term public benefit, centuries before welfare states.

From the moment we wake to the moment we surrender again to the night; we are trying to express something. That expression, whatever form it takes, becomes the quiet architect of our lives. If it aligns with our needs, it becomes a path forward. If it falters, it can cast us into shadows. Creativity, then, is not a luxury. It is the tool we use to shape uncertainty into meaning, and meaning into love.

We are each bearer of dreams, some small, some seismic, all waiting to meet the world. When those dreams find resonance, they become bridges. When they don't, they become burdens. Expression is a need. Creativity is the vessel. And the limits of both are drawn by what we know, until something in us dares to stretch those boundaries.

Dreams are more than illusions of sleep. They are glimpses into a deeper realm, where the self dissolves, and what remains are symbols, urgencies, echoes of unspoken desire. In these states, we are often more honest than in waking life. Our fears step forward without disguise. Our wishes appear in strange, fragmented form. Many have mined this inner terrain for inspiration, seeing in dreams not randomness, but revelation.

Yet dreaming is not without danger. When our expressions fail to land, when our messages are misread or rejected, we suffer. What is a nightmare, if not a dream misunderstood, a failed expression of love?

Consider Theranos, Elizabeth Holmes had a genuine dream of democratizing healthcare through blood testing. But when that expression failed to align with scientific reality, it became a nightmare, not just for investors, but for patients who trusted the technology.

The subprime mortgage market was, at its core, an attempt to express the American dream of home ownership. But when that expression became divorced from economic reality, love became uncertain (families lost homes), hope became haunted (entire communities devastated).

A nightmare is the cry of misaligned meaning. It is the moment when fear wraps itself around longing, and what was once beautiful turns menacing. Love becomes uncertain. Hope becomes haunted. But within even the darkest dreams lies something essential: the reminder that we still care. That we are still reaching. That love, though wounded, remains alive.

This duality, the dance between clarity and confusion, is how we move through the spectrum of knowing. From the silent dark of the unknown-unknowns, into the foggy awareness of the known-unknowns, and finally into the fragile light of the known-knows. We do not leap between them. We stumble, learn, and dream our way forward.

Creativity is our savior when inertia threatens. It takes the fragments of what was, and asks: what else could this mean? What else could this become?

Without it, fear calcifies.

When the COVID pandemic shut down restaurants, those that survived asked those questions. They became grocery stores, meal kit services, virtual cooking classes. The restaurant industry didn't just endure, it transformed.

Even failure can be transformed. Like fire itself, creativity consumes and renews, sometimes destroying what no longer serves, to clear space for what might.

But we are not meant to carry these transformations alone.

Look at how Bitcoin emerged: Satoshi Nakamoto shared a dream of decentralized currency. That dream resonated with others who felt the same need for financial sovereignty. The network grew not through traditional marketing, but through shared meaning-making. Cryptocurrency was an unknown-unknown until Nakamoto's whitepaper. Then it became a known-unknown as people grappled with its implications. Now, with institutional adoption, certain aspects have become known-knows, while new unknowns continue to emerge.

Similarly, the open-source software movement thrives because programmers share dreams of better, freer tools. Linux, Wikipedia,

GitHub, these are economic powerhouses built on collective dreaming and shared expression that initially developed on uncertain ground.

We are vessels, yes, but not without walls. Each of us can only hold so much of the unknown before it overwhelms. That is why love, if it is to grow, must extend beyond the self. It invites us to stretch our arms outward, not only to embrace what we know, but to meet the unfamiliar with tenderness. From the narrow realm of our personal needs, we begin to include others: first family, then friends, then the cities we live in, the nation's we belong to, the world that shelters us all.

Just as love must extend beyond the self to grow, businesses face the same challenge: how to maintain their core identity while expanding to serve broader markets.

This widening of love is not just moral, it is evolutionary. The more fears we confront, the more our circle must expand to contain them. And with each expansion comes a new challenge: how to express clearly across greater distances. How to maintain intimacy when the boundary stretches. How to be understood when language must travel further and pass through more hands.

To love at scale, we must compromise. Not by diminishing our truth, but by offering it in ways others can meet. Expression, in its purest form, is not an act of domination, it is an invitation. A shared bridge over silence. Yet many messages are lost before they ever arrive, scattered by winds of assumption or fear. And so, misunderstanding becomes the shadow side of love. The more diverse the circle, the more effort needed to be seen clearly within it.

McDonald's early international expansion failed spectacularly in several countries because they didn't account for local "grammar of love", the deep cultural meanings around food, family, and gathering. Their eventual success came through compromise, such as offering rice burgers in Taiwan, vegetarian options in India, table service in France. Each adaptation was a form of translation, finding ways to make their core offering resonate across different cultural filters.

Similarly, the dot-com bubble of the late 1990s exemplifies dreams of digital transformation, but many failed because they couldn't translate those dreams into language that traditional consumers could understand, like Pets.com which had a vision, but it arrived through gates they couldn't control or simply consumer behavior patterns that weren't ready for their message.

Compromise is not surrender; it is a survival strategy. In ecosystems, species that cooperate endure longer than those that dominate. In love, too, the willingness to yield is often what allows both to continue.

Linux succeeded where proprietary systems struggled because it embraced collective compromise. No single entity controls it entirely, but thousands of developers willingly shape their contributions to fit the larger whole.

This is why so few expressions are ever fully understood. Even in families, it takes years, sometimes decades, for children to recognize the humor, the pain, and the dreams embedded in their parents' voices. The deep grammar of love is not taught in a moment. It is learned by presence, by repetition, by the invisible thread of attention over time.

Coca-Cola has spent over a century teaching consumers their "grammar", associating their product with happiness, sharing, and belonging. This deep understanding isn't built through advertising alone, but through "presence, repetition, and the invisible thread of attention over time.

When our circle of love encompasses not just individuals but groups, those with different desires, fears, or belief systems, our language must evolve. Sarcasm in one community is truth in another. Reverence in one is ridicule in the next. The meaning we give to our dreams must travel across this landscape of difference, or risk becoming nightmare. Compromise, again, becomes the cost of connection.

Every word we speak, every act of love or silence, passes through countless filters. Each person we meet carries a battalion of past experiences, unspoken traumas, longings, and assumptions. Your message, no matter how well-intentioned, will arrive through a gate you do not control. This is not failure. It is the nature of human contact.

And so, we look for balance, not in perfect understanding, but in sincere exchange. In the willingness to meet each other halfway. In the realization that creation is never born from certainty alone, but from a dance between what we know and what we're still learning to name.

Some will dream more often than others. Some will be more frequently visited by nightmares. This isn't unfair, it is simply the distribution of consciousness across experience. Some hearts carry heavier stories. Others float in lighter sleep. The difference is not a measure of worth, but of rhythm.

Why does this disparity exist? Perhaps it is shaped by how harmoniously one's reality aligns with one's perception. The more deeply someone lives within a shared world of meaning, the more likely they are to dream. The more fragmented, the more haunted. Dreams emerge when our needs find voice. Nightmares when they are strangled by silence.

This explains why some of the most innovative solutions come from the margins, from people whose reality doesn't align with conventional perceptions. Necessity forces them to dream differently, to find new forms of expression.

For love is not just the feeling of affection, it is the impulse to give form to what matters. The act of holding space for the unseen.

The courage to express, even when misunderstood. The resilience to try again, even when your words fall short.

We often think of the individual as the unit of creation. But no one arrives fully formed. We are shaped by others as much as we shape ourselves. We become who we are through encounters, through reflection, through shared survival. Our genius, our dreams, our heartbreaks, none of these exist in isolation. They all depend on the presence of another.

Every act of expression carries cost: the risk of rejection, the energy to translate need into language. But it is a cost we pay because the alternative, silence, is more dangerous. In evolution, what cannot adapt, perishes. And in love, what cannot connect, fades.

The more we open ourselves to that presence, the less we think in purely individual terms. This is not erasure of the self, it is its expansion. But as the nature of the exchange evolves, so too does the composition of the audience. A new balance must be struck between personal expression and shared understanding. And this balance is love's true work.

At the heart of it lies one truth: that compromise, when entered willingly, is not weakness. It is grace. It is the moment when the individual chooses not to abandon themselves, but to shape their message in a form others can receive.

The European Union, despite its challenges, represents this kind of economic grace—nations choosing to compromise their individual sovereignty to create shared prosperity. Each country maintains its identity while adapting to function within a larger economic organism.

Creation does not flourish without presence. Presence is not only physical, it is the unspoken willingness to share space. And love, if it is to take root, requires this first compromise: to be here, now, with intention. Without presence, there is no dream to speak of. Only noise. Only absence.

Consider how Zoom became essential during the pandemic, not because it was technically superior, but because it created a form of shared presence that allowed economic activity to continue. The company understood that commerce requires the unspoken willingness to share space.

The rise of influencer marketing demonstrates this principle. Brands pay creators not just for reach, but for their ability to create intimate presence with audiences, to be "here, now, with intention" in ways that traditional advertising cannot.

Presence is the soil from which all creativity grows. Without it, nothing can take root. Dreams, however vivid, remain unfulfilled without the act of creation. Needs, however deep, remain unmet without expression. What we witness, again and again, is a circular rhythm: presence fuels creation, creation reveals new needs, and love moves between them as both compass and current.

This is not a perfect order, it is a living one. Chaotic, yes. But purposeful. A system built not on symmetry, but on relationship. In this design, dreams are alerts. Needs made audible. Signals from within that demand response. And every response, whether word, gesture, invention, or silence, is a form of creation.

But creation cannot happen in isolation. Not truly. Even the most private work is shaped by the unseen presence of others, by the dreams they once shared, the stories they left behind, the frameworks we inherited from them. The act of expression always carries within it the echo of many voices.

The more intentional our presence, the more clearly, we can hear these echoes. And the more conscious our creativity, the more powerful our ability to transform those echoes into something new.

Yet, even in this beautifully autonomous process, something crucial can go missing: awareness of the initial compromise. When presence is withdrawn, when we show up only half-aware, or not at all—the system falters. Misunderstanding takes root. Love is misread. Creation loses its direction. And what was meant to be a connection becomes a distortion.

This is the quiet tragedy of misused love: when it's offered without presence, when it's expressed without truth. Not all absence is silence. Some of it is noise pretending to be care. Without true presence, even the most poetic act can become a hollow gesture.

But when love is rooted in presence, something extraordinary becomes possible. The individual no longer exists solely as a solitary actor, but as a living signal in a collective dream. Being present, fully, openly, is the first message we ever send. Before we speak, we show up. Before we build, we listen.

And in this, we return to the earliest understandings of identity: that we are defined not by what we own or what we say, but by what we create in response to our needs. Actions, not labels, have always been the truest measure of a life. In ancient times, people carried their acts like sacred tokens. They didn't tell you who they were, they showed you. The weight of their presence was visible in the wake of what they had shaped.

To become a knight was not merely to wield a sword, but to master the language of love. To take action not just from duty, but from feeling. In hardship, they turned inward, to presence, to devotion, to the invisible compass of meaning. Each quest they embarked upon was not only a journey through the world but a declaration of their capacity to love.

This practice, of seeking meaning through noble action is fading in modern life. But it still lives in those who create not for fame, but for alignment. It lives in those who pursue what is difficult because it feels right. It lives in the artists, the caregivers, the builders, the visionaries.

It lives, too, in the entrepreneur.

For in today's world, entrepreneurs are the new knights, defenders of dreams, and architects of belief. They take ideas and give them bodies. They risk rejection, misunderstanding, failure. But they do so in service of something greater than security: the possibility of change. Their currency is not merely financial. It is emotional. It is presence translated into vision.

And when this emotional currency is authentic, when it springs from a real desire to meet shared needs, it often outperforms any established institution. It resonates in ways that traditional power cannot. It sparks belief. It draws others into its circle of love.

But just like the knights before them, these dreamers must know the cost. The wider the audience, the more compromise is required. The more people invited into your vision, the harder it becomes to hold a single voice. You must listen. You must adapt. You must be willing to translate your expression into something others can receive.

This is not selling out. It is scaling love.

The more people a message hopes to reach, the more layered its language must become. Imagine a comedian standing before a vast crowd, hoping to make each person laugh. In that moment, the risk is total. Laughter is the most honest form of agreement. It cannot be faked. It cannot be forced. It is the body saying: "Yes. I see what you see."

To make someone laugh is to make them present.

And that is the great task of the modern storyteller: to lead others to presence. Whether through joy, sorrow, or revelation, the aim is the same. To close the gap between souls. To make the unfamiliar familiar. To turn the unknown into something we can love.

We often speak of logic and reason as if they are the height of our knowing. But beneath our awareness, something older hums. The subconscious—vast, untamed, instinctive guides more than we admit. It is the quiet orchestrator of choices we later call rational. The painter beneath the rational frame.

This subconscious force has evolved for millennia, molded by survival, shaped by trauma, softened by love. And though it hides from view, it is often the very reason we create. Before we can name a need, it pulses through us. Before we can speak a dream, it has already begun its silent forming.

And this, too, is love, though not the soft kind sung in poems. This is love as instinct, as design, as the mysterious compass that pushes us toward others. Toward building. Toward believing. Toward staying.

When this love emerges within a group, it becomes something even greater: a shared dream. A collective expression. And in that convergence, the impossible becomes possible. Communities move. Systems evolve. Visions take shape. But it all begins with presence. With the willingness to meet another where they are, not to conquer, but to co-create.

Ignition Love reveals that economics, like love, is fundamentally about the courage to remain authentic while becoming comprehensible to others. It's about expanding our capacity to hold complexity, to translate across difference, and to find grace in the compromise required for genuine connection.

In both love and economics, survival depends not on perfect understanding, but on the willingness to keep trying to meet each other where we are.

Every person's presence is a message. A signal: "I am here, and I am willing." It is the first, silent compromise. And in that moment, love has already begun.

From there, we build. With each shared moment, each vulnerable offering, each attempt to understand, we construct the foundation upon which something new can live. But the act of creation is never linear. It twists, reshapes, unravels, and begins again. It requires patience. It requires faith. And above all, it requires a kind of surrender to something beyond control.

No system, no relationship, no organization can thrive without love at its core. Not sentimental love, but the love that listens, adapts, and stays curious. The love that seeks to understand what cannot yet be spoken. The love that risks being misunderstood for the chance of being real.

This is why every system changes. Why every structure must eventually evolve or fall. Because love, in its truest form, does not stagnate. It moves. It expands. It includes more. And as it grows, it stretches the boundaries of what is possible.

History shows us this. Again and again, the greatest transformations begin not with certainty, but with longing. Not with systems, but with stories. Not with control, but with courage.

Love fuels this courage. To share a dream. To speak a truth. To build a bridge where none existed. To sit in the unknown without closing your heart. And when love is received truly received, it becomes courage in others. Courage to grow. Courage to listen. Courage to change.

Entrepreneurs know this. Artists know this. Lovers know this. Every human who has ever stood before another with their heart in their hands knows this.

The systems we build will rise and fall. The tools we use will change. But the current beneath it all what drives us, what lifts us, what saves us, is always love. When given, it strengthens. When returned, it expands. And in its light, even the unknown becomes a little less terrifying.

Because love does not eliminate uncertainty. It walks with it.

It does not promise perfection. It offers presence.

It does not guarantee understanding. But it opens the door.

And so, we end this chapter where all beginnings truly begin, not with the mastery of knowing, but with the ignition of care. The willingness to tend a spark. The courage to light the dark. The humility to say: I don't know everything, but I am here.

This is ignition. This is presence. This is love at the edge of the unknown.

Every successful business is ultimately an act of love, a belief that connecting human needs with solutions will create something valuable for the world.

To love is to risk the burn. But from that heat comes creation. We survive not through certainty, but through ignition: that first courageous spark, born from wonder and want, that dares to become flame.

And from here, we step forward into, Conscious Love.

Ignition Love

NECESSITY
Love as function before the first flicker.
Primal need that urges us to reach and survive.

EXPRESSION
Moving from ineffable to intimate.
Giving form to dreams through creative courage.

TRANSLATION
Adapting message to meet others where they are.
Compromise as grace, not weakness.

PRESENCE
Willingness to share space with intention.
The soil from which all creativity grows.

EXPANSION
Widening circle from self to others to world.
Evolutionary imperative to include more in love.

RESONANCE
When dreams find others and become shared vision.
Collective expression that moves communities.

COURAGE
Willingness to tend the spark to light the dark.
Risk of the burn for the creation of flame.

Conscious Love: Presence as Power

In a world where attention is the rarest currency, love begins not with passion, but with presence.

Herbert Simon's groundbreaking work on "bounded rationality" in the 1950s showed that humans don't process infinite information; we "satisfice" rather than optimize because attention itself is limited.

To love is not merely to feel. It is to notice.

It is to give the moment its due weight. To meet reality not as it flatters you, but as it truly is. Conscious love begins not with the heart's racing or the body's yearning, but with attention, the soft and focused flame of being with something, fully. It's a gaze that does not merely see, but witnesses. It's a presence that doesn't just arrive, it remains.

Where Ignition Love is the spark born of instinct and necessity, Conscious Love is what happens when the spark steadies into a lamp. When we learn not only to burn, but to carry the flame through wind and doubt. It is the shift from raw emotion to cultivated presence.

Presence, in this sense, is not physical proximity. You can stand beside someone and still not be with them. Conscious presence means asking the more difficult questions. Not only "What am I feeling?" but "What is this feeling teaching me?" Not "Do they love me?" but "Am I truly seeing them, or only my idea of them?" It is this shift, from projection to perception that births Conscious Love.

But awareness is no passive act. In a world saturated with noise, to attend to something becomes a radical gesture.

Netflix didn't just compete with other streaming services, they competed for the scarcest resource: human attention. Their algorithm isn't designed to find the "best" content, but to capture and hold attention most effectively. Their success came from understanding that in an attention economy, engagement matters more than perfection.

Similarly, the rise of TikTok demonstrates that attention, once given deliberately, transforms both giver and receiver. The platform succeeded because it mastered the art of conscious presence, creating content that doesn't just demand attention but rewards it with genuine moments of connection and discovery.

In economics, scarcity drives value. In the economy of attention, love is the ultimate investment. Behavioral economics teaches us that humans do not always act with perfect rationality. We are drawn to what is immediate, distracted by novelty, driven by impulse. Our attention drifts unless something anchors it. Conscious love is that anchor. It pulls us back, again and again, into presence.

And this pulling back is the practice. We do not achieve consciousness in a single awakening. It does not dawn and remain.

It flickers. It drifts. It forgets. And then, gently, it returns. That return is love.

The most resilient economic systems are those built on sustained attention rather than reactive emotion. They succeed not by avoiding all discomfort, but by remaining present through uncertainty long enough for wisdom to emerge.

Conscious love is the parent choosing patience after the fifth interruption, not because it is easy, but because presence is worth more than irritation. It is the partner who, instead of defending themselves, listens. Not to win, not to fix, but to understand. It is the friend who remembers what you said when you were too tired to mean it as a confession but too honest to hide it.

Warren Buffett's investment philosophy embodies this principle. His famous quote "Our favorite holding period is forever". Reflects the same conscious choice to remain present through market volatility rather than react to immediate impulses.

These quiet moments are unremarkable on the surface, form the root system of lasting connection. They do not demand attention; they offer it. And in doing so, they reshape the relationship. Attention, once given deliberately, transforms both giver and receiver.

Every act of presence says, "You are real to me."

That is not a trivial statement in a world bent on illusion. We are encouraged daily to live in abstraction, to scroll past, to skim, to multitask our way through meaning. Conscious love is a form of resistance. It insists: "I will slow down. I will not look away. I will stay."

But presence also has a cost. We cannot be everywhere. We cannot feel everything. The mind, unlike our dreams, has boundaries. That limitation is not a failure, it is a guide. Conscious love does not ask us to love universally; it asks us to love intentionally. To choose, with clarity, where our gaze will rest.

The Federal Reserve's dual mandate, controlling inflation while maintaining employment demonstrates this limitation. They cannot attend to every economic indicator simultaneously; they must choose where to focus their attention.

Like any finite resource, our attention must be budgeted. Where we spend it shapes what thrives, and what withers.

Behavioral economics calls this bounded rationality, the recognition that humans cannot process all information equally. We operate under constraints. This truth has implications for how love works. We are not made to love everyone in the same way. We are made to love what we attend to most deliberately. Attention is not just the currency of love, it is its shape.

That's why conscious love begins not with grand declarations, but with decisions. The decision to notice. The decision to listen.

The decision to remain in discomfort long enough for truth to emerge.

Discomfort is where conscious love proves itself. Anyone can adore a mirror. But conscious love happens when you sit with someone else's jagged edges, without trying to sand them down. It is the love that does not flinch from contradiction. It holds complexity without rushing to resolve it.

Imagine a healthcare policy written with the attentiveness of a caregiver. Or a school curriculum designed not around test scores, but around listening to what students aren't saying.

This is also the love we must give ourselves.

To love yourself consciously is to reclaim your own attention from shame, from urgency, from the noise of comparison. It is to witness your desires not as commands but as invitations. Conscious self-love is the willingness to see your internal contradictions, your inherited wounds, your messy hopes, and stay. Not to fix everything.

Very often we confuse self-awareness with self-criticism. We think that to notice is to judge. But conscious love tells us something else. To notice in order to embrace your own humanity. To have a conversation with it. To talk to yourself not as an employee, a rival, or someone you do not know - but as someone who is trying every day to remember the light, he/she is.

This is where emotional intelligence takes root. Not in controlling our feelings, but in attending to them. Listening to what envy is trying to tell us. Asking what our silence is hiding. Discovering what joy actually wants when it shows up.

JPMorgan Chase, under Jamie Dimon's leadership, largely avoided the subprime mortgage crisis by practicing what is described as emotional intelligence in economics. They asked difficult questions: "What is this market euphoria teaching us? What are we not seeing?" Their willingness to sit with FOMO (fear of missing out) while maintaining lending standards saved them from catastrophic losses.

When we become students of our emotional lives, we no longer treat relationships as destinations, but as reflections. We stop asking others to complete us and start wondering: What part of myself do I still withhold from presence? What part of myself am I scared to let be known?

Love, then, becomes a place of unveiling. Conscious love reveals. It does not entertain the fantasy of perfection. It builds a sanctuary of permission. You may be flawed here. You may change here. You may speak what you didn't think you could say.

Because conscious love trusts not in the stability of the person, but in the stability of the presence between them. The agreement: "I will keep returning, even when it's hard. Even when you disappoint me. Even when I disappoint myself."

This form of love anchored in attention, steeped in reflection, does something revolutionary: it makes us responsible without making us ashamed.

To love consciously is not just a matter of emotional hygiene, it is a model for how to engage with the world.

Conscious love begins as an internal discipline, but it cannot remain private. Its nature is expansive. What you tend to with care becomes too alive not to spill over. The same attention that heals a wound in one relationship becomes the blueprint for how you build community. Conscious love ripples outward from self, to others, to systems.

A relationship is a system. So is a family. A neighborhood. A workplace. A government. These are not mechanical machines. They are living networks of attention. And wherever attention gathers, love or the lack of it is revealed.

In behavioral economics, it is often said: what is measured, matters. But what is measured is also what is noticed. And what is noticed is what is shaped.

This is why conscious love holds power beyond the personal, it is the seed of social change. Systems are not impersonal. They are structured reflections of where we collectively direct attention. If our institutions fail to serve the vulnerable, it is not because they are broken, it is because they are following the logic of unconscious attention: to favor the loud, the powerful, and the familiar.

Think about Denmark's flexicurity model, combining flexible labor markets with strong social safety nets. It's economically tough (easy hiring and firing) but socially tender (comprehensive retraining and support). This conscious design emerged from attending to both market needs and human dignity.

But when we bring conscious love into the architecture of systems, we reorient that logic. We begin to ask: Who has been ignored? What pain has been normalized? What joy has been delayed too long? These questions are not sentimental. They are structural. They are how healing begins, one noticing at a time.

To love a system consciously is not to romanticize it. It is to look at it honestly and refuse to abandon it. It is to understand that care is not always soft, it is sometimes fierce. That love in public means accountability, persistence, and design.

Rather than simply demanding war reparations (as happened after WWI), the U.S. chose to practice economic presence with former enemies. George Marshall understood that the plan was tough on communist expansion but tender toward European recovery.

It is the work of those who stay in the room after the shouting stops. Those who draft new policies with the same tenderness they use to write a letter to someone they love. Those who understand that love, when it is real, seeks to restore, not just relationships, but realities.

Love that listens also begins to build.

Similarly, the creation of the Bretton Woods system in 1944 represented conscious economic design. John Maynard Keynes and Harry Dexter White didn't just create monetary policy; they built an architecture of attention that would prevent the economic nationalism that led to two world wars.

This is why conscious love is not passive. It is deeply participatory. It shows up, again and again, even when comfort tempts us toward silence. It makes a practice of care, not only in grand gestures but in small, consistent alignments.

It becomes a way of voting, not just on ballots, but with presence. What you pay attention to, you empower. What you neglect, you permit. Conscious love is the quiet protest against numbness, against habitual cruelty, against the erosion of empathy through overload.

It is not a luxury. It is survival.

We often think of survival in the context of food, shelter, and safety, and rightly so. But attention, too, is nourishment. We are not just sustained by calories; we are sustained by recognition. We begin to starve the moment we become invisible, even to ourselves.

In a world overflowing with stimuli, attention is the new scarcity. It is the gold standard of human currency. You cannot manufacture it at scale. You cannot automate it. You cannot fake it for long. This is what makes it so valuable, and so vulnerable to misuse.

The Medici banking empire of 15th-century Florence succeeded not just through financial innovation, but through what you describe I am describing as conscious love, sustained attention to client relationships across generations. Cosimo de' Medici understood that banking required presence, not just proximity. While competitors focused on immediate transactions, the Medici practiced ritualized attention, remembering clients' family histories, cultural preferences, and long-term needs. This conscious approach allowed them to maintain banking relationships across decades and continents, becoming Europe's most trusted financial institution.

Similarly, the Dutch East India Company's 17th-century dominance came from practicing sustained economic presence across vast distances. Rather than just extracting resources, they invested in local infrastructure, learned regional languages, and developed relationships with local rulers. This attention to cultural coherence allowed them to maintain profitable operations for over 200 years.

Conscious love defends attention from commodification. It reclaims it. It says: "My gaze is not for sale. My presence is not content. My love will not be performed for applause." It reorients the economy of intimacy around depth, not breadth.

When you give someone, or something, your real attention, you are investing your most limited resource. More than time. More than money. It is the resource that defines what kind of world you help create.

If you attend only to flaws, you become a cynic. If you attend only to ease, you become complacent. If you attend only to yourself, you miss the miracle of connection.

But when you choose consciously, when you curate your gaze, you begin to craft a life of coherence.

Conscious love matures not through passion but through practice. It does not demand we always feel inspired, it asks that we stay intentional. That we weave our attention into the fabric of the everyday. That we understand that devotion is not a mood. It is a method.

Equally, successful companies like Amazon demonstrate this practice. Jeff Bezos famously said, "We're not competitor obsessed, we're customer obsessed." This reflects the shift from what we think customers want to actually listening to what they need.

This is where love becomes ritual.

Not a performance, but a rhythm. A way of returning, again and again, to what matters most. A way of saying, even in stillness: I am here. Conscious love shows up in the morning voice you use with your child. In the way you touch your partner's back without asking for anything in return. In the way you send the text that says, "I remembered."

The Champagne region of France developed ritualized attention to terroir , weather patterns, and aging processes that created irreplaceable economic value.

Dom Pierre Pérignon, the Benedictine monk credited with improving champagne production in the late 1600s, exemplified conscious love. He practiced daily return to presence, tasting grapes from individual vineyard plots, adjusting blending techniques based on subtle seasonal variations, and maintaining detailed records across decades. This sustained attention created a luxury market that persists 300+ years later.

Love does not grow by volume. It grows by depth. And depth is born from attention sustained over time. From the moments that could be skipped but aren't. From the conversations that are hard, but chosen anyway. From the apology offered before being asked. From the witnessing of someone else's truth, even when it confronts your own.

The guild system of medieval Europe institutionalized this conscious approach as well. Master craftsmen in cities like Nuremberg and Venice didn't just teach techniques they transmitted attention practices. The seven-year apprenticeships were exercises in sustained presence, creating coherence between word and action, intention and impact.

This kind of love is not thrilling in the way fireworks are. It is the candle that stays lit through storms.

Conscious love does not scale by breadth, it deepens by deliberate repetition.

And when enough of these candles burn together, they illuminate more than relationships. They illuminate meaning. We begin to understand that love is not just something we feel. It's something we build. With language. With memory. With trust. With discipline.

And most of all, with attention.

—

Let us return to the economic metaphor, because here the resonance becomes undeniable: attention is not just a personal resource; it is a shared economy. What you give attention to affects not only your own reality but others' too. You amplify what you attend to.

Viscount Charles Townshend and other agricultural reformers, instead of extracting maximum short-term yield, they developed rotation systems that sustained soil fertility across decades. This conscious choice launched the Agricultural Revolution and supported England's population growth through the Industrial Revolution.

In today's economy algorithms know this. Media campaigns know this. Politics knows this. So, the question becomes urgent: Do you?

Conscious love demands we become stewards of this resource. Not to hoard it. Not to manipulate it. But to honor it. To offer it where it can do the most good and not where it gives us the easiest dopamine hit.

To love consciously is to know that the quality of your attention defines the quality of your relationships.

Two people may spend a lifetime beside each other, yet never meet. Proximity does not equal presence. Presence is what makes the difference between being looked at and being seen, between being heard and being understood. And this, more than anything, is what we are all searching for, not love as possession, but love as recognition. Love that says: I see you. And I am still here.

In this light, even conflict becomes sacred. It becomes a place not for ego to win, but for truth to emerge. When practiced consciously, disagreement does not break love, it deepens it. Because in conscious love, the goal is not to win, but to understand. Not to dominate, but to reveal.

The Hanseatic League, a medieval trading confederation spanning Northern Europe from the 13th to 17th centuries, institutionalized economic disagreement among competing merchant cities. Rather than eliminating competition, the League created structures for conscious economic conflict, shared trading standards, dispute resolution mechanisms, and collective defense agreements. Cities like Lübeck, Hamburg, and Bergen competed fiercely while maintaining cooperative frameworks. This balance of competition and collaboration created one of history's most successful trading networks.

This requires courage. To love consciously is to choose discomfort over illusion. It is to let go of needing to be right so you can be real. It is to speak honestly even when your voice trembles, and to listen with an open heart even when what you hear hurts.

And it is in this ongoing exchange that this rhythm of revealing and receiving and that intimacy is born. Not from perfection, but from coherence. From the alignment of word and action, intention and impact, promise and presence.

This alignment builds trust. And trust is what allows love to endure, not just in romance, but in family, in friendship, in community. Trust is not built through intensity. It is built through consistency, even in small things.

The Rothschild banking network of the 19th century demonstrates how trust is built upon this concept. Starting with Mayer Amschel Rothschild in Frankfurt, the family built Europe's most influential banking empire not through dramatic gestures but through methodical attention to information flows and relationship maintenance.

You start to realize: conscious love isn't always exciting. Sometimes, it's quiet. Sometimes, it's inconvenient. Sometimes, it's a question you ask even when you already know the answer, just to say: I care enough to ask again.

The more honest we are with ourselves, the more compassion we can offer others. For if you have sat with your own contradictions, your own disappointments, your own longings, you will not turn away from theirs. You will recognize them. And you will stay.

This staying power, this maturity of attention, is the true expression of conscious love. It is what transforms fleeting connection into trust. It is what allows relationships to be romantic, familial, and communal, to deepen. To last.

The Hudson's Bay Company, founded in 1670 and still operating today, illustrates sustained economic attention across centuries. Their success in the fur trade came from practicing conscious love with Indigenous communities, learning languages, respecting cultural protocols, and maintaining trading relationships across generations. This approach contrasted sharply with competitors who used extractive, transactional methods.

Conscious love does not seek only compatibility. It seeks coherence, between word and action, between desire and discipline, between intention and impact.

And this coherence ripples. It spreads outward from the individual into every layer of life. Into how you hold space. Into how you disagree. Into how you lead. Into how you leave.

Eventually, you realize that this is not just about how you love others. It's about how you love the world. It's about whether your presence builds or breaks, connects or divides, amplifies or silences. It's about whether your love has weight, whether it is made of more than wanting.

And if you reach this place, this rare place of stillness and intention, then the path forward becomes clear.

The Toyota Production System, developed in post-WWII Japan, demonstrates conscious love in manufacturing. Taiichi Ohno and Eiji Toyoda created what they called "respect for people", systematic attention to worker knowledge and continuous improvement. Rather than treating employees as interchangeable parts, Toyota practiced their presence by listening to worker suggestions, investing in training, and maintaining long-term employment relationships.

This approach contrasted with Henry Ford's earlier assembly line model, which prioritized efficiency over human attention. However, Toyota's conscious approach eventually revolutionized global manufacturing creating a more sustainable competitive advantage.

To love consciously is to step into your worth. To recognize that your value is not given, but remembered. Not offered by others, but claimed within. It is to say: I am no longer seeking love to define me. I am choosing love to express me.

This, then, is the bridge to what comes next.

Not the love that burns wild or waits patiently, but the love that stands tall.

The love that knows its name.

The love that is not afraid to take up space, to declare meaning, to form identity.

The love that is worthy.

The more you practice conscious love, the more it begins to change your very sense of self. Because what you pay attention to shapes what you believe, and that includes what you believe about you.

As you choose presence again and again, you begin to soften toward yourself. You start to see your patterns not as verdicts, but as signals. You stop measuring your worth in outcomes. You begin to recognize the quiet power of simply staying aware of letting the mirror be honest, and still remaining in front of it.

Conscious love, then, becomes a sanctuary. Not a place where you are always comfortable, but one where you are always welcome. You stop waiting to be fixed, and start learning to be faithful, to your truth, to your growth, to your presence. You realize that your value is not given by the gaze of others, it is restored by the gaze you offer yourself.

And so, your love deepens. Not because it becomes more performative, but because it becomes more aligned. You stop chasing experiences that are loud, and start building a life that is real.

When Japanese electronic watches threatened Swiss mechanical watchmaking, the industry could have simply competed on price and functionality. Instead, companies like Rolex, Patek Philippe, and Audemars Piguet chose to express their identity—craftsmanship, tradition, and mechanical artistry. This shift from seeking market approval to expressing core values created the modern luxury watch market.

When this kind of love is extended to others, it ceases to be conditional. You no longer ask: "What will I get from this?" You begin to ask: "What will I bring to this?" The relationship becomes less of a transaction and more of a vessel, for growth, for healing, for creation.

You learn to love in ways that liberate rather than bind. You create space where others can unfold, not into what you want, but into who they truly are.

This is the moment when conscious love reaches its full strength, not when it holds tightly, but when it holds truly. Not when it becomes everything, but when it allows everything to be.

And this clarity, this rooted presence, leads us to the next horizon.

Because once you've learned to be present, not only with others, but with your own needs, fears, longings, contradictions, you begin to ask deeper questions. You begin to sense that love is not only something to give, or something to feel, but something to embody. To become.

Conscious love shows us that whether we're discussing medieval guilds or modern organizations, the same principles apply: economic systems thrive when they practice presence over proximity, coherence over intensity, and stewardship over extraction.

That love, in its most coherent form, is the way we stand. The way we speak. The way we declare our identity in a world that asks us to forget it.

It is from this ground that we step forward and not into a louder love, but into a love that knows its name.

A love rooted not just in attention, but in worth.

A love that dares to say:

"I do not seek love to define me. I offer love to express who I already am."

And that, dear reader, is the beginning of the third movement: Worthy Love, the love that stands tall, that forms identity that creates belonging through clarity and integrity.

Let us walk there, into the realm of Worthy Love.

Conscious Love

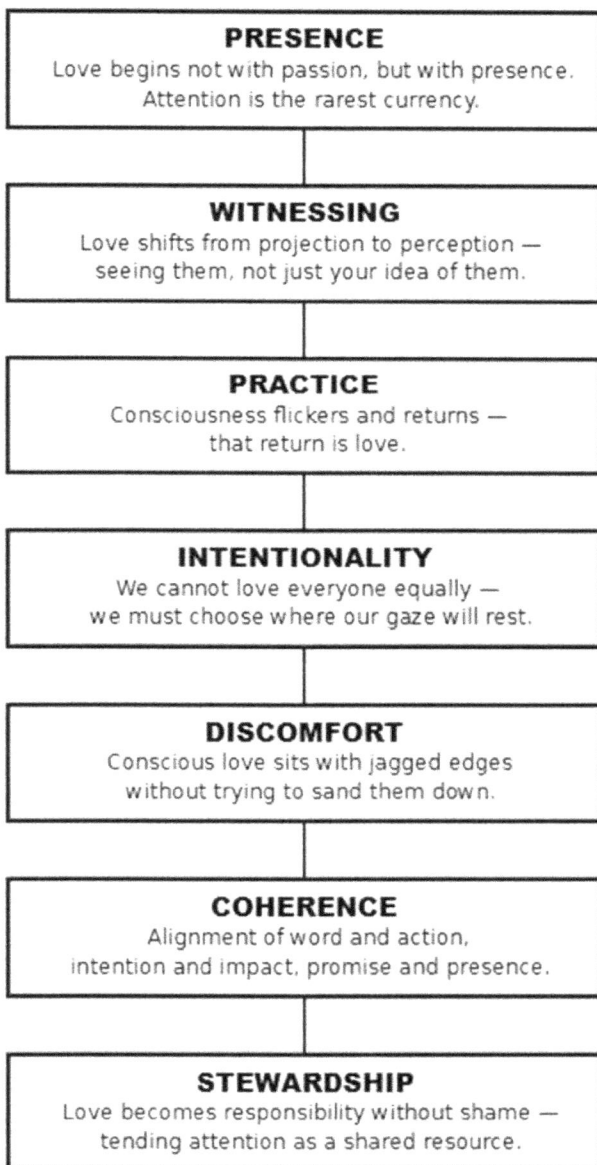

PRESENCE
Love begins not with passion, but with presence.
Attention is the rarest currency.

WITNESSING
Love shifts from projection to perception —
seeing them, not just your idea of them.

PRACTICE
Consciousness flickers and returns —
that return is love.

INTENTIONALITY
We cannot love everyone equally —
we must choose where our gaze will rest.

DISCOMFORT
Conscious love sits with jagged edges
without trying to sand them down.

COHERENCE
Alignment of word and action,
intention and impact, promise and presence.

STEWARDSHIP
Love becomes responsibility without shame —
tending attention as a shared resource.

Worthy Love: Identity and Integrity

There comes a moment in the journey of love where the questions change. Not because we find all the answers, but because we finally stop asking the wrong ones. We stop asking, Am I enough? Do they see me? Will they choose me? And instead, we begin to ask, what do I stand for? What kind of love do I offer when no one is watching?

This is the turning point. It's quiet. Often invisible to others. But inside, it changes everything.

Worthy love begins when love stops being something we chase and becomes something we stand in. It does not seek permission. It does not wait for validation. It is not shaped by someone else's recognition. Instead, it rises from within, built on a kind of dignity that doesn't depend on applause.

Companies like Cadbury, Rowntree, and Barclays Bank were founded by Quakers who refused to compromise their values for profit. They practiced business as an expression of identity rather than mere wealth accumulation. Cadbury's refusal to use slave-produced cocoa, even when it was cheaper, reflected worthy love, maintaining integrity regardless of market pressures.

This kind of love does not perform. It does not bend itself into palatable shapes to be accepted. It does not shape shift to fit the expectations of others. It no longer waits in the wings of someone else's stage. Worthy love steps forward and says, this is who I am. This is what I carry. This is what I will not compromise anymore.

Many of us begin our lives offering love with open hands and open hearts, not knowing that our worth has already been made into a negotiation. We are praised for being agreeable, for making others comfortable, for staying small. We learn that love is safest when we please. We learn that to be chosen, we must shape-shift, shrink, and soften our edges.

And so, for years and sometimes for decades, we do. We offer our love as proof of our usefulness. We perform kindness as a down payment for being kept. We stay silent when something hurts because the silence seems safer than loss.

But all the while, a quiet ache grows. The ache of self-abandonment. The slow erosion of our inner compass. We lose track of where we end and others begin. And eventually, something within us begins to whisper, there must be more than this.

Worthy love begins when we finally listen to that whisper.

It begins when we stop treating love as a reward and begin to recognize it as an expression. It is the moment we reclaim ourselves, but instead of fury, we reclaim ourselves, with clarity. Not with force, but with truth.

To love from worth is not to love less. It is to love cleaner. Love without hooks. Without hidden contracts. Without the small print of "please don't leave me" buried under every gesture.

Worthy love does not cling. It does not audition. It does not spend energy trying to convince another person of our value. It already knows that value is not a thing to be negotiated. It is a thing to be remembered.

This remembering is quiet, but it is radical.

It changes how we speak. We begin to say what we mean, rather than what will be liked. We begin to listen not to respond, but to understand. We stop performing love as currency and begin to live it as truth.

Reflect on IBM's dramatic pivot in the 1990s under Lou Gerstner. The company had to abandon its old identity as a hardware manufacturer and embrace its true strength, services and consulting. This wasn't just a business strategy change; it was worthy love, choosing to express their actual capabilities rather than clinging to outdated market perceptions. The transition was painful, requiring layoffs and cultural transformation, but it saved the company.

This kind of love is not loud. It is not always romantic. Often, it is the love that says no when yes would cost too much. It is the love that walks away from what once felt like safety when safety becomes a cage. It is the love that finally chooses peace over proximity.

In the food industry, In-N-Out Burger has maintained worthy love for over 70 years by refusing to franchise or expand beyond their quality control capabilities. While competitors like McDonald's pursued rapid growth, In-N-Out choosing "peace over proximity" and maintaining their standards even if it meant slower expansion. This approach has created one of the most beloved restaurant brands in America.

Worthy love is not driven by scarcity. It is not fueled by the fear of being alone. It is not a desperate grasping. It is not the love that says, "Please stay so I can feel like I matter."

Instead, it is the love that says, "Even if you leave, I will not leave myself."

This is not easy. It is not romantic in the way we're taught love should be. There is grief here. Letting go of old patterns means mourning old selves. Sometimes it means disappointing people who were used tso the unworthy version of us—the version that gave endlessly, spoke softly, asked for little.

But that mourning is necessary. Because what comes after it is a love with a spine. A love that does not collapse under the weight of someone else's needs. A love that knows its shape and keeps it.

Worthy love builds boundaries not as barriers, but as invitations. It says, "This is the shape of who I am. If you want to meet me, come here, don't ask me to disappear to make you comfortable."

The luxury goods industry validates this clearly. Hermès has maintained a waiting list for their Birkin bags for decades, not due to artificial scarcity but because they refuse to compromise their artisanal production methods. Their boundary, we will not mass-produce, becomes an invitation to customers who value exclusivity and craftsmanship. This "love with a spine" has made Hermès one of the world's most valuable luxury brands.

And slowly, things begin to shift. We stop being attracted to what drains us. We stop mistaking intensity for intimacy. We start choosing people and places where we don't have to explain our value, it is already seen.

Our relationships change. Not always by ending, but by reorienting. Some connections will fall away. Others will deepen. Not because we fought to keep them, but because we finally stopped fighting ourselves.

And here's the most liberating truth: the more rooted you become in worthy love, the less you need to be understood by everyone. The less you need your worth reflected in every mirror. You stop chasing belonging. You start becoming it.

Worthy love becomes a compass. A filter. A foundation. It changes how we show up, not just in romantic relationships, but in friendships, families, communities. It changes how we spend our time, how we make decisions, how we use our voice.

And it begins to ask a different question, not "Will I be chosen?" but "What am I choosing to create?"

This shift from seeking to standing is the soul of worthy love. And once you've made it, the world no longer feels like a courtroom. It becomes a canvas.

Disney's evolution under Walt Disney shows this transformation. Rather than simply competing in the entertainment industry, Disney created an entirely new category, family entertainment that appealed to both children and adults. Walt's worthy love for animation and storytelling, combined with his refusal to compromise on quality, transformed Disney from a small animation studio into a global cultural force.

Worthy love is not an idea, it is a discipline. It is a way of living. And like all forms of disciplined love, it begins with attention.

Attention is not just what we offer to others. It is what we give to ourselves. Every time we choose to notice our needs instead of ignoring them, every time we speak what's true instead of swallowing it, every time we rest instead of pushing through, these are acts of worthy love. They are how we begin to live like we matter.

You can tell a lot about someone by how they use their attention. Not the curated kind offered to the public, but the quiet kind like the attention they give to their own joy, to their own anger, to their longing. Worthy love knows that those things are not inconveniences, they are messengers.

To live from worth is not to become selfish. It is to become centered. It is to stop leaking energy in every direction, trying to prove your value to people who cannot hold it. It is to begin channeling that energy into a life that reflects you.

This is the slow reclamation of your time. Your space. Your voice. And perhaps most of all, your permission, to take yourself seriously.

Worthy love is serious. Not heavy, but sacred. It does not treat life like a joke. It does not treat pain like performance. It treats your presence as something consequential.

Because once you believe your life matters, everything changes.

You stop tolerating what drains you. You stop over-explaining to those committed to misunderstanding. You stop offering your love like a discount, available to anyone who asks for it, regardless of whether they can receive it.

And you start offering love from fullness, not fear. From clarity, not desperation.

You begin to choose people not for their potential, but for their patterns.

You stop hoping that one more explanation will earn your respect. You start paying attention to how people act when you say no. You begin to believe that "difficult" does not mean "wrong." That "alone" does not mean "unworthy." That "peaceful" does not mean "boring."

Worthy love teaches you how to live without apology.

Not without mistakes. Not without accountability. But without apology for your existence, your needs, your rhythms, your depth.

It teaches you that boundaries are not proof of distance, they are the structure in which trust is built.

That honesty is not cruelty. Instead it's clarity.

That soft does not mean weak, and firm does not mean cold.

That silence can be sacred, but it can also be complicity.

That your intuition is not irrational, it is your earliest language, and you would do well to relearn it.

And eventually, this kind of love reshapes the internal dialogue. The cruel editor that once narrated your life, always cutting you down, always finding flaws, begins to quiet. In its place comes something slower, kinder, and more rooted.

The voice of your own becoming.

That voice doesn't always sound confident. Sometimes it still trembles. Sometimes it still asks for reassurance. But it doesn't abandon you anymore. It walks with you.

And when you learn to walk with yourself, you no longer fear walking away.

Worthy love is what allows you to leave what no longer honors you. Not with rage, not with shame, but with grace. You no longer stay where your presence must be negotiated every day. You no longer perform for scraps. You no longer ask for the bare minimum.

You no longer shrink.

You start to see your love not as a currency to be traded, but as a current to be channeled. And when that current flows in alignment, it nourishes. It uplifts. It creates.

This is where something beautiful happens. Worthy love stops being just a personal revelation. It becomes a force of design.

Because the more rooted you are in your own worth, the more aware you become of the systems around you that don't reflect it. You begin to notice where love is distorted in culture, in how people are trained to doubt themselves, to tolerate harm, to silence their knowing. You start to see the outlines of a world built on unworthiness.

And worthy love refuses to reinforce it.

You stop participating in conversations that diminish people. You stop laughing at things that require someone else to be the punchline. You stop consuming stories that normalize emotional starvation. You stop pretending that busyness is virtue, that burnout is proof of effort, that perfection is the goal.

When Patagonia ran a full-page ad in The New York Times on Black Friday saying "Don't Buy This Jacket," they embodied this refusal to participate in systems of diminishment. They chose to challenge over consumption culture even though it could cost them sales, because worthy love in business means refusing to profit from what harms the whole.

Worthy love doesn't want you perfect. It wants you whole.

It begins to reshape how you lead. How you create. How you parent. How you partner. How you make decisions. You stop asking, what will make me look good? And start asking, What will make me feel aligned?

Ben & Jerry's consistently chose alignment over optics, maintaining a 5:1 salary ratio between executives and workers, using their ice cream cartons as platforms for social justice messages, and refusing to compromise their values even when it meant turning down lucrative opportunities. They asked not "How will this look?" but "Does this reflect who we are?"

And this, this is the subtle revolution.

Because the more people begin to live from worth, the more the culture around them must adapt. The systems built on shame begin to crack. The expectations built on silence begin to shake. The institutions that rely on performance without presence begin to feel thin, transparent, breakable.

When Buffer published everyone's salaries, their revenue numbers, and even their struggles publicly, they cracked open the tech industry's culture of secrecy. Their transparency forced other companies to examine their own practices around pay equity and authentic communication. One company's commitment to worthy love created ripples throughout an entire industry.

Worthy love doesn't just change the lover.

It changes the world the lover moves through.

And in that shift, something structural begins to awaken.

A new question emerges, not just, how do I love well? But how can love be built into the world around me?

This is where the personal becomes systemic.

But before we step into that next chapter, before we start talking about how love can inform our structures, our institutions, our economies, we have to fully live this one.

We have to be able to say: I no longer need to be loved in a way that costs me myself. I will not bend to be digestible. I will not disappear to be chosen. I will not decorate my wounds so they seem less disruptive.

I will love as I am. From worth. From clarity. From a place that does not beg to belong but knows it already does.

The more fully you stand in your own worth, the less willing you become to distort love for the sake of harmony. You stop confusing peace with appeasement. You no longer keep quiet just to avoid tension. You begin to understand that tension is not something to fear, but it's something to feel.

And when you can feel discomfort without collapsing, love becomes honest.

Worthy love is not always comfortable. It's not about keeping everything calm and unchanging. It is about staying true when things change. It is about holding your center when everything around you pulls for compromise.

This is where integrity comes in, not as a lofty ideal, but as an everyday practice. Integrity is simply coherence between what you feel, what you say, and what you do. Worthy love is integrity embodied. It no longer allows the mind to say yes when the heart says no. It no longer permits the soul to be silenced by convenience.

That integrity gives your life shape. It makes you more trustworthy, to yourself and to others. It creates a kind of emotional gravity. People feel it in your presence. You become someone who doesn't need to be perfect, but who is clear. Someone who doesn't speak over others, but also doesn't disappear.

This kind of presence is rare. And in its rarity, it becomes a quiet invitation. It doesn't demand others match your depth. But it offers them the permission to. It creates a kind of relational clarity: this is who I am. This is where I stand. This is how I love. If you want to meet me here, you can.

But I will not chase. I will not beg. I will not plead for understanding that costs me my voice.

That shift, from persuasion to presence, is one of the deepest markers of worthy love.

Because when you live from this place, your relationships begin to feel different. They aren't just emotional exchanges anymore. They become collaborations. They become spaces of truth. Spaces where both people are allowed to be seen, not only for their beauty, but also for their rough edges. Not only for their usefulness, but for their reality.

Worthy love invites a kind of maturity that moves past transaction. It is not what do I get from you? But what do we get to build, now that we are both standing whole?

In this space, love is no longer measured by proximity, performance, or permanence. It is measured by how much truth it can hold. By how much growth it can welcome. By how much silence it can sit with, without becoming fragile.

You stop asking: Will this last forever?

You start asking: Is this alive now? Is this healthy now? Are we still growing here?

This is the evolution of love. From fixation to freedom. From control to collaboration.

And sometimes, worthy love means leaving. Not out of bitterness. Not out of avoidance. But out of respect, for yourself, and for the truth of what a relationship has become. Not every love story is meant to be lifelong. Some are meant to be doorways. Some are meant to be catalysts. Some are meant to teach us what love is not.

But worthy love knows that leaving can be sacred. That endings can be honest. That departure does not mean failure.

You no longer stay because you're afraid to start over. You no longer keep holding what no longer holds you. You know the cost of staying too long in places where your truth must be hidden to be accepted.

And so, you make space, for something new, yes, but also for your own return.

Worthy love is not just about who we love or how we love others. It is just as much about how we come home to ourselves. Again and again. Through heartbreak. Through transitions. Through reinventions.

It is the willingness to walk with yourself when everything falls apart. The discipline to tell yourself the truth, even when no one is asking. The strength to rebuild, not to become who you used to be, but to become more of who you really are.

And as that version of you begins to emerge, unapologetic, grounded, soft but firm, you begin to realize something: your love is no longer about you alone.

Because when your love is rooted in worth, it becomes sturdy enough to carry more than just personal desire. It begins to carry intention. Vision. Design.

You begin to ask: What would the world look like if it were shaped by this kind of love? Not the grasping kind. Not the anxious kind. But the grounded, discerning, liberating kind?

You begin to see the connections between how we treat ourselves and how we treat others. Between what we accept in our personal lives and what we allow in our systems. You begin to sense that worthy love is not just a feeling, it is a foundation.

A foundation upon which things can be built: relationships, yes, but also families, teams, communities, movements, structures.

William Lever built Port Sunlight not as a factory town but as a community. Workers received houses with gardens, libraries, schools, and healthcare, not as charity but as recognition of their inherent worth. Lever believed that business success built on worker degradation was hollow. He constructed an entire town on the foundation that human flourishing and business prosperity were inseparable.

You start to feel the architecture of it. Not as control, but as coherence.

You realize that love is not just about hearts and connection, it is about culture. About systems. About power. And that the first revolution is always internal.

Worthy love prepares us for this. It stabilizes us, so we can stabilize others. It teaches us how to stand firm without closing our hearts. How to stay open without abandoning ourselves.

When the 1906 San Francisco earthquake hit, most banks refused to lend to immigrants and working-class victims. A.P. Giannini set up a desk on the waterfront and lent money based on character, not collateral. His "Bank of Italy" (later Bank of America) was built on the radical premise that banking should serve "the little fellow." He refused to participate in systems that excluded people based on class or origin.

From here, the personal starts to turn into the political. The emotional becomes structural.

But before love can become a system, it must first become a practice. A way of being. A way of relating. A way of seeing the world not as something to survive, but as something to shape.

Worthy love is a form of design. Not design as decoration, but as foundation. When you love from a place of worth, you begin to design your life from alignment, not compensation. You are no longer trying to "make up for" something, your past, your pain, your perceived flaws. You are no longer living to fix the version of you that someone else once misunderstood. You are no longer managing your life like a crisis. You are building it like a temple.

This is a holy turning point.

Because once you stop constructing your world from survival, you begin to build from sovereignty. That changes everything. The way you work, the way you rest, the way you partner, the way you show up to conflict, all of it begins to reflect your inner order.

And this inner order doesn't require approval. It doesn't need to be constantly defended. It doesn't depend on whether others agree. It simply is.

When Henry Ford doubled wages to $5 a day in 1914, he cracked open the industrial assumption that workers were disposable. Critics called it foolish, but Ford saw his workers as potential customers, not just costs. By paying dignity wages, he created a consumer class that could afford his cars. One company's refusal to build on worker poverty helped create the modern middle class.

This is the quiet power of worthy love: it stabilizes you in a world that is often unstable. It roots you in truth when the noise tries to confuse you. It keeps you oriented, not because you always know what to do, but because you know who you are.

From here, love matures. It becomes less about being seen and more about seeing. Less about being accepted and more about being clear. Less about intensity and more about intention.

You no longer need every connection to become something. You no longer need people to match your pace. You no longer feel compelled to prove anything. You have nothing to hide, and nothing to prove. That is freedom.

And when you're free, love becomes an offering, not a transaction.

It becomes a current of generosity—not a contract of mutual insecurity.

It becomes an atmosphere—not just an emotion.

You begin to think in terms of resonance, not relevance. Alignment, not achievement. You ask: Does this feel like truth? Does this honor what I value? Can I stay connected to myself while I stay connected to you?

And if the answer is no, you know what to do.

You don't need permission to walk away. You don't need consensus to feel clear. You don't need a dramatic exit—you simply step back into your own lane, and keep moving.

In this, worthy love makes you lighter. Not because you carry less, but because you carry differently. You carry without the weight of pretending. Without the armor of people-pleasing. Without the illusion of control.

You carry what's yours to carry—and you let the rest go.

And here's the beauty: this doesn't make you cold. It makes you kinder. Because when you are no longer performing, you can finally connect. When you are no longer posturing, you can finally listen. When you are no longer trying to be impressive, you can finally be present.

When Richard Sears introduced "Satisfaction guaranteed or your money back" in the 1890s, it was revolutionary. Most retailers operated on caveat emptor—buyer beware. But Sears asked not, "How can we avoid returns?" but "How can we build genuine trust?" This alignment with customer dignity, not just customer acquisition, built the largest retailer in America.

Presence is the fruit of worth.

When you believe in your own value, you no longer need to dominate a room. You can sit quietly and still radiate influence. You can disagree without being defensive. You can let people be wrong about you. You can stand in a storm and still hold peace.

Worthy love turns your attention outward again—but not in desperation, not in search of something to complete you. Instead, you begin to ask: What can I contribute from this place of wholeness?

This is where love becomes legacy. Because now your love is not only about healing you—it's about building something for others to stand on. You begin to notice the structures around you. You begin to see where worth is missing, and how much damage that causes. You begin to ask: What would it look like to build spaces, systems, relationships, and cultures where people are treated as already worthy?

Not because they've earned it.

Not because they've proven anything.

But because worth is not something to win. It is something to protect.

This is where the personal becomes systemic. When your love grows strong enough to begin shaping the world around you.

Worthy love becomes the architecture behind how you create. Behind how you parent. Behind how you lead. Behind how you build.

It becomes the lens through which you evaluate opportunity—not Will this make me successful? but Will this make me proud?

Not Does this look good? but Does this feel aligned?

Not What can I get from this? but What does this ask me to become?

And then, you begin to organize your life differently. You start to set up your relationships, your time, your work in a way that reflects not just who you are—but what you believe.

George Pullman built an entire town around his railcar factory—complete with schools, libraries, parks, and model homes. Though his paternalism had complex motivations, Pullman recognized that worker dignity required more than wages. He built physical infrastructure around the belief that human flourishing and business success were interconnected, creating a template that influenced industrial town planning for decades.

Worthy love becomes culture. Quietly, slowly, steadily. You stop chasing environments to fit into. You begin building environments that fit your truth.

It shows us that true economic success comes not from being chosen by everyone, but from clearly expressing what we stand for and attracting those who share our values.

This doesn't mean you always get it right. You will still falter. Still compromise. Still forget sometimes. But the difference is, now you come back faster. You come back cleaner. You come back without shame.

Because you've made an agreement with yourself. And that agreement is this:

I will not treat my worth as negotiable.

I will not make myself small to be safe.

I will not distort my truth to be kept.

I will love without bargaining.

I will stay with myself—even when it's hard.

This agreement becomes your North Star. The one thing you do not leave behind.

And from this place—finally, fully—you are ready.

Ready to love at scale.

Ready to move from love as a feeling into love as design.

Ready to explore what it means to embed love into systems.

To treat care as structure.

To honor people, not just in theory, but in architecture.

This is where we go next.

Into Systemic Love. Where love becomes practice. Where presence becomes policy.

Worthy Love

RECLAMATION
Love stops being something we chase and becomes something we stand in.

EXPRESSION
Love shifts from reward to expression — this is who I am, what I will not compromise.

BOUNDARIES
Boundaries become invitations — this is my shape, meet me here.

INTEGRITY
Coherence between what you feel, what you say, and what you do.

DISCERNMENT
Choose people for their patterns, not their potential.

SOVEREIGNTY
Build from sovereignty, not survival — your life becomes a temple, not a crisis.

ARCHITECTURE
Worthy love becomes design — building spaces where worth is protected.

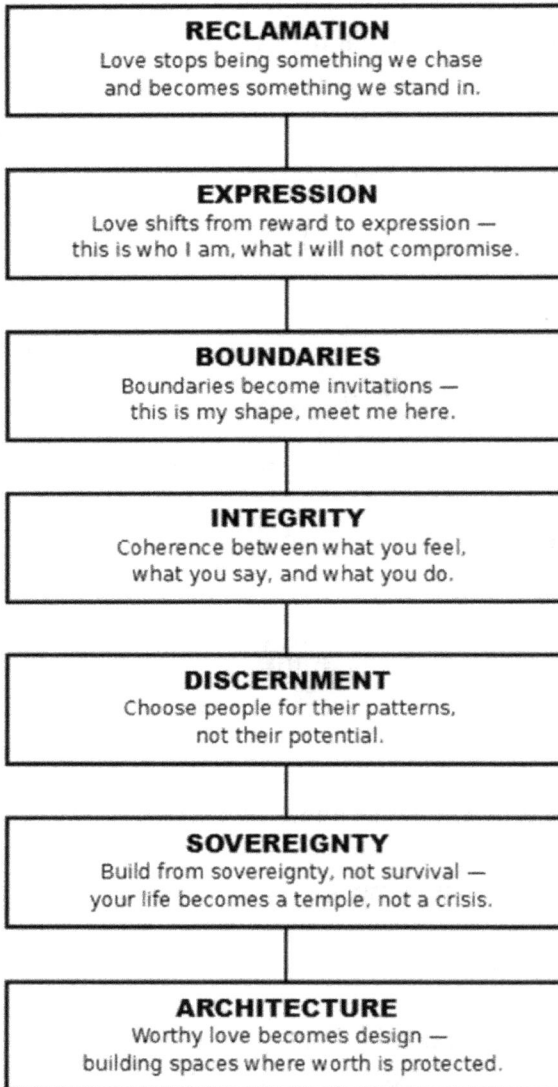

Where the worth we've reclaimed internally becomes the blueprint for everything we choose to build.

Systemic Love: Love Embedded in Structures

Systemic love begins where personal love grows too large to stay inside one person.

Love, at its most enduring, is systemic—a force that shapes the architecture of belonging, the choreography of interdependence, and the rhythms of collective care. It is not a moment, but a momentum. It moves through everything.

It's what happens when care stops being confined to intention and starts informing structure. When love ceases to be just a private value and becomes a public ethic. When you no longer ask only, How do I love well in my life?—but also, What would a world built on this love look like?

We often treat love as a personal matter—intimate, quiet, domestic. But love, like power, is never just personal. The way we love—or fail to—shapes the systems we build. And the systems we live inside either reflect love or distort it.

Sears president Julius Rosenwald used his business success to build over 5,000 schools for African American children across the segregated South. What began as one man's conviction that education was a human right became a systematic challenge to Jim

Crow. His "Rosenwald Schools" educated a generation of Black leaders, showing how systemic love becomes institutional change.

Systemic love is not abstract. It is not poetic metaphor. It is the most pragmatic, tangible, and enduring form of love: the kind that gets written into policies, woven into design, expressed through leadership, embedded in contracts, organizations, education, and infrastructure.

If worthy love is how we claim ourselves, systemic love is how we create the world that reflects that claim. It's the practice of building lives, teams, communities, and institutions around the premise that people—as they are—are worthy of care, dignity, and protection.

It asks not, How do I feel about you? but, What conditions have I created to make care sustainable?

When Lincoln Electric promised no layoffs in 1958, they weren't making a feel-good gesture—they were building systemic care into their business model. For over 60 years, through recessions and industry upheavals, they've kept that promise by designing flexible systems: cross-training workers, maintaining cash reserves, and sharing profits. They created conditions where care wasn't dependent on good times—it was the foundation that sustained them through bad ones.

To understand this deeper dimension of love, we must pull the lens back. Beyond private moments and personal passions lies a larger, pulsing world. Systems. Patterns. Institutions. Networks of unseen forces that govern how we live, work, connect, and care. If love is truly to matter, it must matter here too. It must shape not only how we feel but how we build.

Life itself is a constellation of systems—some visible, others hidden beneath the surface. There are personal systems: how we manage time, energy, identity. There are familial systems: rituals, roles, rhythms that form our earliest understandings of care. There are societal systems: laws, customs, economies. Each is composed of feedback loops, constraints, structures, and shared meaning. And within each, love either flows or falters.

Systemic love is not sentimental. It is strategic. It understands that affection, if not supported by access, equity, and structure, becomes a fleeting sensation instead of a sustaining force. To truly be systemic, love must account for the complexity of the environments we live in. It must reckon with histories of exclusion, patterns of inequality, and structures that were never built for everyone to belong.

Consider education. A child's capacity to learn is deeply shaped by the systems surrounding them: the quality of their school, the safety of their neighborhood, the nutrition of their meals, the stability of their caregivers. No amount of individual passion for learning can compensate for a system that makes survival a full-time job. If love exists in that child's life, it must be scaffolded by a system that supports their growth, not sabotages it.

This is what separates systemic love from situational affection. It does not rely on mood. It does not rely on proximity. It does not depend on whether I like you. It is built on principles—on the steady, unfashionable disciplines of structure, clarity, equity, and access.

This love lives in how we write contracts.

It lives in who gets to speak and who gets heard.

It lives in which behaviors are rewarded, and which are quietly tolerated.

It lives in the difference between saying "we care" and building systems that care when no one is watching.

Most systems, whether formal or informal, are not built on love. They are built on efficiency. Control. Competition. Legacy. Fear. A scarcity mindset that assumes there is not enough to go around—not enough time, not enough credit, not enough belonging.

But what happens when we challenge that assumption?

What happens when we design from the belief that care is not a finite resource—it's a multiplier?

Systemic love begins with that question.

It recognizes that power without love becomes domination—and love without structure becomes sentimentality. It is not enough to feel care; we have to embed it. We have to design it. We have to make it operational.

Now consider the workplace. A company may proclaim values of inclusion, innovation, and compassion. But if its hiring practices replicate bias, if its leadership only mirrors power, if its incentives reward output over well-being—then systemic love is absent. Love must be traceable in process. It must leave evidence in the policies we write, the data we collect, the budgets we pass.

When Polaroid discovered their instant cameras were being used for South African apartheid identification cards, they didn't just issue a statement—they systematically restructured their entire South African operation. They stopped sales to the government, funded Black education, and redirected profits to anti-apartheid organizations. Love became traceable in their budget lines, their personnel policies, and their supply-chain decisions.

When people are told they matter, but the structures punish rest. When inclusion is a marketing slogan, but all decisions happen behind closed doors. When values are posted on walls but contradicted in practice. This is what happens when love is spoken, but not systematized.

Systemic love refuses the performance of care. It demands embodiment. It does not settle for optics. It looks under the surface:

Who gets access? Who gets safety? Who gets margin for error? Who is asked to give more than they receive? These are love questions. Systemic love asks them early and often.

George Eastman didn't just give his factory workers jobs—he gave them ownership. In 1912, he distributed a third of his own Kodak stock to employees, making thousands of workers instant shareholders. He systematically asked: Who gets to benefit when the company succeeds? His answer restructured the fundamental relationship between labor and capital, creating one of America's first broad-based employee-ownership programs.

Because the health of any system—a team, a family, a nation—is not measured by how it treats its most powerful, but by how it holds its most vulnerable. Love, at this level, becomes governance.

It lives in feedback loops that encourage truth without punishment. It lives in compensation models that reflect respect, not exploitation. It lives in calendars that honor rest as productive. It lives in leadership that prioritizes psychological safety over perfection.

The famous Hawthorne Studies began as efficiency research but revealed something deeper: workers' productivity increased simply because management was paying attention to their concerns. Western Electric systematized this insight, creating regular feedback sessions, worker councils, and open communication channels. They built a system where being heard was as important as being productive—and discovered the two were inseparable.

It begins small. Systemic love doesn't require a revolution overnight. It requires an intentional commitment to bring care into the mundane. To ask love not just to inspire, but to inform.

While other oil companies built exploitative company towns, Standard Oil of New Jersey designed theirs around worker dignity. They provided healthcare, libraries, recreational facilities, and quality housing—not as paternalistic control but as systematic investment in human flourishing. They measured success not just by oil production but by infant mortality rates, literacy levels, and community stability in their towns.

At the individual level, we all carry a personal economy. This isn't just about finances—it's about capacity. It's about the energy you have to give and the clarity with which you give it. Like all economies, it's governed by trade-offs. If you are drained, love feels scarce. If you are aligned, love feels abundant. Managing this economy—what the Greeks called "oikonomia," or household stewardship—is the first step toward system-level love. Because you cannot serve what you cannot sustain.

When our inner economy is balanced—when attention is aligned with purpose, when energy is replenished rather than depleted—we create space where love can flourish without the weight of chaos or confusion. This internal order becomes a kind of compass, guiding decisions, relationships, and investments of time. But as our circle of care expands—when we partner, parent, collaborate, lead—our systems grow more complex. More variables. More inputs. More interdependencies. And with that, more opportunity—and more risk.

We start asking different questions in meetings:

- Who wasn't in the room?

- Who made the decision, and why?

- What unspoken norms are we protecting?

- Are we making it easier or harder for people to thrive here?

We begin to reimagine policies:

- What would this look like if we assumed everyone was trying their best?

- How do we make it safe to speak up?

- Are we building systems that make burnout the price of excellence?

- Are we designing for inclusion, or just inviting people into systems not built for them?

These are not "soft" questions. These are the bones of sustainable leadership. The scaffolding of real belonging. The design language of love.

Because love—when systematized—becomes culture. It becomes pattern. It becomes predictive. People don't have to guess whether they are safe, whether they are seen, whether they are valued. The system tells them.

And when it doesn't, they know it's not personal—it's structural. And that means it can be addressed. Not with blame, but with intention.

This is the great power of systemic love: it depersonalizes pain without denying it. It shows us that suffering is often not the result of one person being cruel—but of systems designed without care. And it calls us to do better.

Not because we feel guilty.

But because we have learned to love well enough—and clearly enough—to want better for others, even when it costs us comfort.

Systemic love begins to reveal itself in the small decisions—the ones that seem too ordinary to matter. Who gets to interrupt? Who is expected to stay late? Whose needs are framed as individual and whose as organizational?

These are the subtle spaces where power lives. And where power lives, love must also live—or distortion fills the gap.

Without systemic love, even the most well-intentioned relationships eventually collapse under the weight of accumulated neglect. Without structure, love becomes exhausting. Without clarity, inclusion becomes chaotic. Without equity, care becomes conditional.

This is why systemic love cannot be improvised.

This is the domain of systemic love—where love evolves beyond the relational into the architectural. Here, love becomes both a design principle and a maintenance ritual. It's no longer just about good intentions. It's about systems that carry those intentions forward with integrity, even when no one is watching.

Any company survives through transactions—payroll, products, meetings. But it thrives through relationships—trust, communication, care. A well-oiled machine can still feel cold if its processes lack warmth. Similarly, an organization that runs on vision but neglects structure quickly burns out. Systemic love is the bridge: it unites the transactional with the relational. It ensures that the mechanisms of productivity are infused with humanity.

And it's not just organizations. Entire communities function this way. They require both scaffolding and soul. Streets must be paved, yes—but so must stories. Trash collected, but also grief shared. Housing provided, but also hospitality offered. A community thrives when it allows for both ritual and repair.

When a healthcare system centers patient dignity, it tells a story: you are not just a case file—you are a whole human being, worthy of time and tenderness. When a criminal justice system prioritizes restoration over retribution, it tells a story: people can change, harm can be healed, community can hold more than punishment.

This is where we often go astray. When systems become overly transactional, we lose the thread. Bureaucracy replaces belonging. Policy replaces presence. And slowly, people begin to disengage— not because they don't care, but because they no longer feel cared for. On the other hand, if systems are too relational without structure, they collapse under the weight of ambiguity. Emotional labor without boundaries turns to burnout. Goodwill alone cannot carry the load.

The art, then, is in the balance. Systemic love is not the opposite of order—it is the soul of sustainable order. It asks: How can we make care durable? How can we embed dignity into design?

Let's be clear: love, in this context, is not a soft virtue. It is an organizing principle. It is as concrete as budgets and blueprints. It is encoded in the way we write laws, structure meetings, allocate resources. It shows up in who gets heard, who gets helped, and who gets held when things fall apart. Love is the invisible ink in every operating manual that values humanity above mere functionality.

Charles Nash understood this in 1916 when he shared 10% of Nash-Kelvinator's profits with every employee. This wasn't generosity—it was systematic recognition that love becomes operational when workers become stakeholders, not just wage-earners.

We see this truth in rituals—collective moments that reinforce shared purpose. Graduation ceremonies. Weekly dinners. Mourning vigils. These are not just traditions. They are systems of remembrance. They reinforce what matters and who matters. They are emotional infrastructure, keeping the connective tissue of society alive.

And yet, systemic love does not stop at culture. It must reach into design. Into policies, workflows, architecture, budgets. Love must be able to pass through channels that do not depend solely on personality. It must be scalable. It must endure. Systemic love, then, becomes an ethic of continuity—a way of ensuring that our best values survive our worst days.

This is especially urgent when we consider scale. The larger a system grows—be it a company, a school district, a nation—the more brittle it becomes when love is not embedded. Growth, if unmanaged, often prioritizes efficiency at the cost of empathy. That's why systemic love is not a luxury. It's a form of risk management. It's how we prevent disconnection, disenchantment, and decline.

Metropolitan Life grasped this in 1909 with their Visiting Nurse Service, providing healthcare to entire families of policyholders. They understood that an insurance company's health was inseparable from community health—so they systematically invested in both.

We saw it when disaster struck and neighbors turned into lifelines. When strangers became shelters. When mutual aid networks emerged faster than official relief. When teachers created makeshift classrooms in kitchens and on porches. When people gave not because they were told to, but because love compelled them to act. That is systemic love in motion.

But we don't need a crisis to build such systems. We only need clarity and commitment.

Systemic love requires a shift from extraction to reciprocity. From "What can I get?" to "What can we grow together?" It changes leadership—not as domination, but as stewardship. The leader who listens first. The boss who builds feedback into every process. The policymaker who codes humanity into legislation.

James Cash Penney embodied this in 1902 by making store managers partners rather than employees. His systematic approach to shared ownership transformed how people showed up to work— when everyone has skin in the game, stewardship becomes natural.

It also reimagines power. Power not as something to hoard, but something to share. Systemic love sees power as a tool—not to control, but to uplift. Not to silence, but to amplify. This kind of power makes room. It redistributes. It multiplies by giving.

And make no mistake: this is hard work. It requires us to confront our habits of convenience. To question inherited norms. To trade simplicity for nuance. But in return, it gives us systems that do more than function—they flourish.

The flourishing system is one where teachers are trusted, not just tested. Where healthcare treats the soul as much as the symptom. Where policies are written with the people they affect. Where design thinks in generations, not just quarters. Where the invisible work of care is made visible, valued, and shared.

Such a system doesn't pretend to fix everything. But it does promise one thing: no one is forgotten. No one is disposable. No one is loved only when they're useful.

That promise changes everything.

It shifts how we show up in meetings. How we write emails. How we run companies. How we parent. How we grieve. How we dream.

Because the dream of systemic love is not utopian. It is deeply practical. It's about building everyday systems that do not break us. That don't ask us to choose between efficiency and empathy. That don't treat burnout as a badge of honor. That don't expect mothers to mother alone. That don't abandon the aging. That don't criminalize difference.

It's about a world where care is not the exception—it's the rule.

Systemic love insists that systems be responsive to the full range of human experience: joy and grief, triumph and trauma, confusion and clarity. It makes space for all of it.

But here's where the metaphor deepens.

Imagine society as a body. Love is not the heartbeat—it is the blood. It moves through every vessel. It nourishes the organs. It delivers oxygen to the places most often forgotten. It heals wounds from within. And if the flow is obstructed—by inequality, neglect, indifference—the system suffers. Disease spreads. Disconnection takes root. But when love flows freely, the body thrives.

So how do we build systems that love?

We start small.

We embed care in our calendars. We add pause into our agendas. We invite feedback, and mean it. We ask: Who is missing from this table? and What might make them feel safe to speak? We hold open doors longer. We build frameworks for forgiveness. We design for return—so that even those who leave in pain know they are still welcome back.

We use our systems not to exclude, but to include more justly. We stop rewarding urgency at the cost of reflection. We stop over-celebrating outputs and begin honoring insight. We see that every spreadsheet reflects a story. Every policy contains a promise. Every process encodes a worldview.

This is systemic love: the recognition that nothing is neutral. Every design choice—conscious or not—carries a value. Every system either strengthens or severs connection. Every structure either expands belonging or contracts it.

Even economics—the most technical of systems—is saturated with human assumptions. Behind every pricing model is a philosophy. Behind every tax code, a theory of justice. Behind every hiring rubric, a vision of worth. Behavioral economics tells us that attention is our scarcest resource. Systemic love asks us to spend that attention not just on efficiency, but on equity. Not just on performance, but on purpose.

Consider how indigenous gift economies operated for millennia on principles that market economics dismisses as inefficient. In potlatch ceremonies of Pacific Northwest tribes, wealth was measured not by accumulation but by how much one could give away. The more a leader distributed—blankets, food, tools—the higher their status rose. This wasn't charity; it was systemic love made economic. The circulation of gifts created webs of relationship that bound communities together through reciprocity rather than debt. When crisis struck, these networks became survival systems. The "inefficiency" of giving everything away became the ultimate efficiency for collective resilience.

When crises come—and they always do—they test whether we've built systems of care, or merely systems of control. Whether we've valued resilience over rigidity. Whether love was treated as decoration or as infrastructure.

Because systems built with love don't just survive storms—they evolve through them. They learn. They adapt. They carry us through the rupture without collapsing.

And that design begins with the decision to take love seriously—not just as a feeling, but as an operating principle. Not just as something we owe to friends and family, but something we owe to one another in every form of collaboration.

Because systems are everywhere. Some are official—companies, schools, governments. Some are informal—friend groups, creative partnerships, co-living arrangements. In all of them, love becomes visible when it begins to shape behavior, access, protection, and possibility.

Love, when embedded into systems, becomes predictable safety. It makes trust scalable. It makes kindness normal, not exceptional.

Modern time banks operate on this principle of systemic love translated into economic practice. In these systems, one hour of anyone's time equals one hour of anyone else's—regardless of skill, education, or social status. A lawyer's hour consulting equals a gardener's hour weeding, equals a storyteller's hour entertaining children. This isn't naive equality; it's systemic recognition that everyone's contribution to community has inherent worth. Time banks create economies of care where love becomes the currency, and the "exchange rate" is always dignity.

This is not to say that systemic love is always easy or always "kind" in the soft sense. Sometimes, systemic love must be fierce. Sometimes it must set boundaries, name harm, end things. But even then, it moves with clarity—not revenge. With justice—not domination. It does not humiliate. It does not retaliate. It restores where possible and protects where necessary.

In systems designed with love, conflict is not hidden or avoided—it is integrated. Feedback is not a threat—it is a tool. Leadership is not the performance of control—it is the stewardship of care.

Systemic love understands that when people feel safe, they take risks. When they feel valued, they tell the truth. When they feel seen, they create. And this is not just good for morale—it's good for outcomes. For innovation. For strategy. For sustainability.

Love is not just moral—it is practical.

Let's talk about leadership. Leadership that lacks systemic love often confuses direction with domination. It treats silence as agreement. It rewards exhaustion. It uses fear as fuel. The result? Turnover. Disengagement. Quiet resentment that becomes louder than any mission statement.

But leadership that flows from systemic love? It listens. It adapts. It builds systems that don't rely on heroes, but on collective clarity. It understands that the job of leadership is not to be the smartest in the room—it is to make the room wise together.

This kind of leadership is not soft—it is precise. It doesn't indulge everything. It sets limits. It names tension. But it does so while holding dignity at the center. It ensures that correction does not equal humiliation. That discipline does not mean dehumanization. That high standards don't come at the cost of mental health.

This is the nuance that systemic love requires: the ability to hold complexity. To design systems that allow people to stretch without snapping. To measure success not just in metrics, but in the emotional health of those doing the work.

Solidarity economy networks demonstrate this complexity in action. These interconnected webs of cooperatives, credit unions, community land trusts, and mutual aid societies operate on principles that seem to violate everything we've been taught about competition and scarcity. When one cooperative struggles, others don't see opportunity—they see obligation. Resources flow not toward highest profit but toward greatest need. Success is measured not by individual accumulation but by network resilience. This isn't utopian idealism; it's systemic love made practical through economic design that prioritizes collective thriving over individual winning.

Consider how economic activity mirrors this pattern: production creates goods not solely because someone wants them but because they fulfill shared desires within a network rooted in trustworthiness—and ultimately driven by love's imperative to create value alongside necessity's demand for survival needs handled efficiently through transactionality.

However—and here lies the crucial insight—the danger emerges when transactional mechanisms become detached from the relational roots they were meant to serve only temporarily—or worse yet—when they replace genuine connection altogether under the guise of efficiency or control.

In such cases, love risks becoming commodified—a mere exchange rather than an ongoing relationship imbued with meaning—and thus losing its transformative power at both personal and systemic levels.

To counteract this drift toward superficiality requires conscious effort—a deliberate weaving together of transactionality with deeper relational intentions:

• Embedding care into every exchange,

• Recognizing mutual vulnerability,

• Cultivating authenticity amid routine,

• Fostering shared narratives that reinforce collective purpose, all contribute to nurturing what I call "systemic love"—a resilient network capable not only of surviving shocks but evolving through them.

Every system—whether it realizes it or not—is telling a story about love. These stories are embedded in the values it promotes, the behaviors it rewards, and the structures it upholds. A family that discourages honesty teaches a child that love depends on compliance. A school that prizes obedience over creativity sends the message that love must be earned through performance. Workplaces that glorify overwork while ignoring healthy boundaries equate love with self-sacrifice. And justice systems that focus more on punishment than repair communicate that love must be deserved, not simply given.

These stories leave a lasting imprint. They shape not only how individuals perceive others but also how they come to understand themselves.

The concept of systemic love calls us to rewrite those narratives. This isn't about surface-level changes like new slogans or rebranding efforts—it's about reimagining the very frameworks our systems are built on. It means creating new foundations: more inclusive hiring practices, more thoughtful incentive structures, healthier feedback loops, and more compassionate ways of relating to one another. It's about cultivating environments that uphold humanity, regardless of someone's role, title, or productivity level.

Imagine a culture where rest is seen as a necessity rather than a luxury. Where emotional expression is valued as insight, not dismissed as weakness. Where policies aim to uphold dignity, not just avoid risk. Where leaders take responsibility not only for outcomes, but for repair. Where conflict is navigated without shame. Where diversity is embraced as a core design principle rather than an inconvenience.

This vision isn't a fantasy—it's a form of love expressed at scale. And it doesn't require a leadership title or formal authority to begin. It starts with the decision to take responsibility for the spaces we influence, however small. It asks us to consider: what kind of environment am I contributing to? What messages about love, belonging, and worth are being communicated through our practices and norms?

Feminist economists have long pointed out that our entire economic system depends on invisible care work—the cooking, cleaning, child-rearing, elder care, and emotional labor that makes all other work possible. If we valued this work at market rates, it would dwarf the GDP of most nations. But because it's performed mostly by women, mostly unpaid, mostly out of love, it remains economically invisible. Systemic love would make this work visible, valued, and shared. It would recognize that the economy of care is not separate from the market economy—it is its foundation.

To work with systemic love is to act with care, to design with dignity in mind, and to redefine success in terms of presence and humanity—not just productivity or profit. Our systems will always mirror what we believe about people. If we believe that people are worthy of love, capable of change, and deserving of compassion, then our designs—our cultures—must reflect that.

Love at scale becomes a design challenge. That design, when practiced consistently, becomes culture. Over time, culture becomes legacy.

This is the work ahead. It does not require perfection—but it does require intention.

To love systemically is to commit: to building with care, to managing with purpose, to leading with empathy, and to never prioritizing efficiency at the expense of humanity.

And when enough people choose to work this way—not once, but over and over again—the systems begin to shift. Not all at once, and not without resistance. But they do change—because love is not just a feeling.

It's the blueprint for how we build the world.

Systemic Love

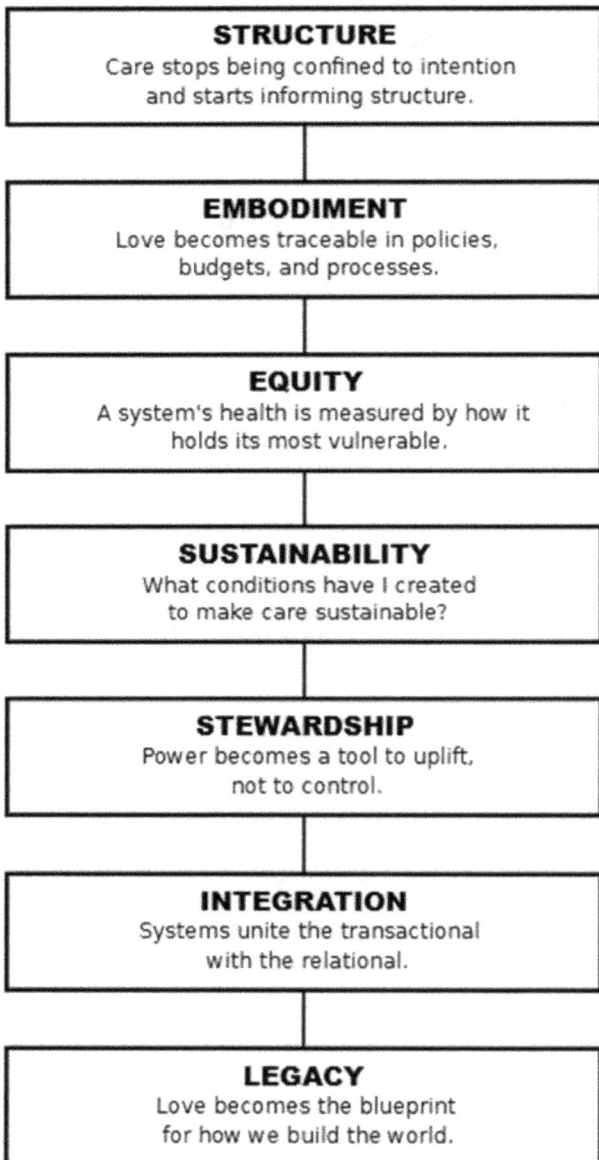

STRUCTURE
Care stops being confined to intention
and starts informing structure.

EMBODIMENT
Love becomes traceable in policies,
budgets, and processes.

EQUITY
A system's health is measured by how it
holds its most vulnerable.

SUSTAINABILITY
What conditions have I created
to make care sustainable?

STEWARDSHIP
Power becomes a tool to uplift,
not to control.

INTEGRATION
Systems unite the transactional
with the relational.

LEGACY
Love becomes the blueprint
for how we build the world.

Relational Love: Mutual Understanding and Empathy

Love is usually pictured as a fragile filament, gently and tenaciously interwoven into the texture of our lives. It seems to shine with an almost diaphanous glow, as if it's something natural, random, and almost magical—that it just happens on its own whenever and however it pleases. However, just beneath this delicate surface is a scaffolding infinitely more complicated than one who merely grazes the surface could imagine: a scaffolding of relationships, conscious choices, and shared dreams that unite people regardless of their time and place.

To truly understand love as a service, one must look beyond fleeting emotions and recognize it as an active, ongoing process of exchange. It is an ever-evolving dance, where compromise, trust, and mutual creation become the rhythm and melody that guide each step.

Love's true essence cannot be encapsulated by passive affection or the simplistic notion of transactional exchanges seeking only stability or comfort. Instead, its vitality springs from its remarkable capacity to adapt and evolve through deliberate, conscious effort. Like a river winding through the landscape, love flows around obstacles rather than battering against them with brute force; it shifts its course gently when necessary, continually seeking harmony within its environment. This fluidity is the hallmark of genuine relational love, distinguishing it from mere mimicry or superficial attachment—those hollow echoes that might imitate the sound of love but fail to nourish growth or deepen connection. Where mimicry is static, genuine love breathes and grows, shaped by the evolving contours of shared life.

When we conceptualize love as a service, it compels us to confront the profound reality that relationships operate much like dynamic systems—interconnected, crowdsourced networks where influence radiates beyond direct, personal interactions. Each individual's choices, emotions, and actions ripple outward, weaving into the collective consciousness of their communities and shared experiences. Love, then, cannot be contained or isolated; it thrives only through active participation and mutual investment. It is a living ecosystem, dependent on the interplay of countless micro-moments, intentions, and gestures that together form a resilient whole.

From the moment of birth, humans begin to experience love not simply as reactive urges or instinctual attachments but through acts imbued with growing intentionality. Newborns do not inherently love what others love or grasp the complexities of social bonds; they are initially driven by basic impulses—curiosity about their surroundings, attachment to the warmth and safety of primary caregivers. Over time, however, these attachments mature and expand. What began as instinctual responses to care evolves into conscious desires fueled by creative acts—disruptions of routine, playful exploration, and the deliberate seeking of novelty. This transformation is no accident but a vital process where curiosity becomes intentionality, and passive reception gives way to active co-creation of relational meaning.

Social media and dating apps create micro-investment opportunities, where small amounts of attention and emotional energy can be deployed across many potential relationships, with the hope that some will generate significant returns on investment. Like emotional smart contracts, relationships develop automated protocols that execute predetermined responses to specific emotional triggers, creating more efficient and predictable patterns of support and boundary-setting.

This innate drive for novelty and exploration feeds directly into our pursuit of fulfillment. Love propels us forward toward desired outcomes, even amid uncertainty, because it carries hope within its core—the profound belief that transformation is possible when guided by purpose-driven action rooted in shared dreams. Love becomes an energetic current, channeling emotional responses toward the realization of our deepest aspirations. It is, in essence, the personal energy powering collective progress—a force that transforms isolated individuals into collaborative communities capable of dreaming and building futures together.

Yet, this journey toward realization rests on understanding a fundamental truth: without risk, love loses its vitality. It stagnates, becoming a mere echo trapped within the boundaries of familiar patterns and known-knows. Love that refuses to embrace risk becomes inert, confined within the comfortable walls of routine rather than engaging actively with the unpredictable complexities of life. To remain alive, love must dare to reach beyond certainty, to push into uncharted territories where vulnerability and growth coexist.

To embrace risk is to acknowledge that love is not a static possession but a living, breathing process that requires constant attention and courage. Without this willingness to venture beyond the safety of the familiar, love withers, turning into a brittle structure held together only by habit and resignation. This truth resonates far beyond personal relationships and echoes clearly in the world of organizations and enterprises, where the same dynamics play out on a larger scale.

Consider the cautionary tale of corporate failure such as Fresh & Easy. This business collapse is not merely about mismanagement or bad timing; it serves as a vivid metaphor for what happens when relational understanding is ignored or undervalued. Fresh & Easy, despite its promising start, failed because it invested heavily in transactional certainty—assuming that a proven model in one market could simply be transplanted into another without deep engagement with local cultural preferences or consumer behavior.

This neglect of the relational fabric between brand and customer led to disconnection, alienation, and eventual collapse. The company's overconfidence blinded it to subtle shifts in its ecosystem, and its rigid commitment to an unchanging formula prevented necessary adaptation.

As communities develop stronger relational infrastructure, they sometimes experience "emotional gentrification," where the rising standards of emotional intelligence and communication make it difficult for newcomers to afford entry into established social networks.

Similarly, Xerox's struggle highlights the perils of defensive complacency. Focused on protecting its existing market share against known competitors, Xerox failed to perceive the nuanced ways in which customer relationships were evolving. Emerging players like Canon and Ricoh succeeded not by brute force but through a refined understanding of niche customer needs and adaptive relational intelligence. These competitors nurtured their bonds with clients through innovative, flexible approaches that resonated with shifting demands. Xerox's failure to embrace relational dynamics rendered its strategies obsolete, revealing a critical lesson: sustained success depends less on rigid rational decision-making and more on an ongoing capacity to read and respond creatively to the subtle shifts within one's ecosystem.

This pattern is not limited to businesses; it reflects a universal principle about the nature of connection and survival. Clinging too tightly to once-successful formulas breeds inertia, which over time ossifies into constraints. These constraints restrict the flexibility needed to navigate an ever-changing landscape. The same way organizations defend strategies long past their usefulness, relationships can become bound by dogma—habits and expectations that no longer serve the shared purpose but persist because of fear: fear of loss, fear of admitting failure, fear of stepping into the unknown. Such collective attachments, rooted more in comfort and control than in genuine growth, slowly strangle the vitality of love.

Love without risk mirrors this rigidity: it becomes a bond maintained by familiarity rather than a living connection that actively embraces change. Such relationships, lacking the resilience forged through adaptation, become vulnerable to external disruptions—whether those come as unexpected challenges, evolving personal needs, or shifts in circumstance. Resilience, the capacity for renewal through deliberate adaptation, is the key to enduring love. It requires the courage to confront discomfort, to loosen the grip on certainty, and to realign continually around a shared purpose that transcends mere habit.

In this dance of relational resilience, control over others' dreams remains elusive. True influence arises not from dominance but from alignment—when one shapes their own narrative in harmony with those around them, forging identity within a collective vision.

Emotional energy becomes a conduit for channeling beliefs into shared reality. Beliefs, far from being arbitrary constructs, act as lenses through which individuals perceive and interact with the world, grounded in genuine resonance with inner truths and social context alike. They provide temporary certainty, a foothold amid chaos, yet true strength emerges only when these certainties are understood as provisional—open to revision through ongoing dialogue with loved ones and community members who challenge and support growth.

In this light, love reveals itself as a form of currency—one that transcends mere transactional exchange to become symbolic capital invested over time. These investments inspire trustworthiness within circles bound by common dreams and aspirations. When honored through consistent commitment and authenticity, these relational deposits accumulate, creating robust bonds capable of weathering inevitable depreciation caused by external shocks or internal doubts. Indigenous communities across Latin America have long practiced "minga"—reciprocal labor networks where community members contribute work to collective projects without monetary exchange. When someone needs to build a house, harvest crops, or repair infrastructure, the community responds not because of formal contracts but because of accumulated relationship capital. The person who helped with last season's harvest can call upon that network when their own needs arise. This isn't barter—it's relational currency where the "exchange rate" is measured in sustained care, presence, and mutual investment in each other's dreams.

What may appear as erosion or wear is, in truth, a natural process of evolution that, when met with renewal efforts anchored in shared purpose, sustains the relationship's integrity. The ancient hawala system demonstrates this symbolic capital in action. For over a millennium, this Islamic financial network has moved billions across continents without contracts, collateral, or even written records—operating purely on trust and relationship. A merchant in Cairo can transfer money to Karachi through nothing more than a phone call and a promise. The "hawaladars" stake their family honor, their community standing, their entire social fabric on each transaction. This isn't naïve trust—it's systematic relationship-building that makes formal banking infrastructure unnecessary. The currency isn't money; it's accumulated credibility that appreciates through consistent service to the network.

This deeply relational model finds a modern echo in the world of software-as-a-service (SaaS), where value also flows through trust, responsiveness, and networked credibility. Like hawala, SaaS platforms rely less on rigid structures and more on fluid, adaptive relationships—between developers, users, and the wider ecosystem. Sustained success in both systems hinges on attentiveness, continual iteration, and the delicate balancing act of maintaining coherence while scaling intimacy across complex, ever-evolving networks. Those who master this balance navigate ongoing feedback loops to recalibrate and nurture their networks in ways that honor individuality while preserving unity.

Muhammad Yunus revolutionized microfinance by recognizing that the poorest borrowers had something more valuable than collateral—social capital. His Grameen Bank lends to groups of women who guarantee each other's loans not through money but through reputation. If one woman defaults, the entire group loses access to credit. This creates a web of mutual accountability where financial success becomes inseparable from relational integrity. The bank doesn't just lend money—it invests in the social fabric that makes repayment possible. Default rates remain below 2% because love, expressed as collective responsibility, becomes the most reliable form of insurance.

Communities function as automated market makers, providing liquidity for emotional exchanges. When someone needs support, the community pool provides immediate access to care, with the understanding that they'll contribute back when others need assistance. In practice, sustaining such enduring bonds hinges on managing two key factors simultaneously. First, lowering entry barriers to ease participation in one's "dream network" by reducing unnecessary transaction costs while ensuring sufficient relational depth for genuine connection. Second, fostering intimacy without sacrificing scalability—balancing minimal compromise against maximum coherence among diverse participants. This delicate trade-off is not a one-time achievement but an ongoing process, navigated only by those willing to continuously listen, adapt, and invest energy thoughtfully.

Depreciation—the inevitable natural wear and tear on collective understanding—is manageable when core values are upheld and unnecessary compromises minimized. Just as meritocratic markets reward those who invest energy wisely, relationships thrive when participants actively reduce uncertainty for one another. Energy itself becomes a currency intimately linked to commitment and trust. From this perspective, love's inherent desire for growth amid constraints transforms into an economy of emotional investment and renewal, a vibrant cycle sustained through relational service.

Ultimately, love transcends the realm of fleeting emotion and becomes an active service—a system designed for continual renewal in the face of uncertainty. It is a resilient architecture, capable not only of enduring inevitable declines but also of reimagining and reinventing itself through incremental change grounded in trust and shared purpose. Love is no longer merely something you feel; it becomes something you do.

This transformation is fundamental. To truly master relational love is to shift from passive reception toward intentional cultivation. Like engineers designing systems for efficiency and endurance, those committed to relational love orchestrate connections with precision and care. They understand that relationships are dynamic, living entities—complex networks that require ongoing maintenance, recalibration, and innovation to remain vital across the shifting landscape of time.

The artful orchestration of relational love is a dance of hearts committed together, weaving resilience into the fabric of connection. Each gesture, each act of listening, each moment of vulnerability and trust functions as a deliberate investment into this system. It is through such acts that love becomes a dynamic engine, fueling not only individual heartbeats but also the collective dreams that propel human survival forward on every scale.

Elinor Ostrom's research revealed how communities successfully manage shared resources—forests, fisheries, grazing lands—without falling into the "tragedy of the commons." These systems work not through top-down regulation but through evolved relationship structures where long-term thinking trumps short-term extraction. Fishermen in Turkish coastal villages, for example, develop intricate systems of rotation and mutual monitoring that ensure everyone benefits while preserving the resource for future generations. The "currency" here is multi-generational relationship capital—the understanding that today's restraint becomes tomorrow's abundance, but only if the community bonds hold strong enough to delay gratification collectively.

This journey toward relational mastery invites us to embrace paradox and complexity—to hold certainty lightly while committing deeply; to risk vulnerability even when faced with the fear of loss;

to innovate constantly without losing sight of foundational values. It demands courage, creativity, and humility.

And yet, in this ongoing act of relational service, love offers profound rewards. It reveals itself as the ultimate connector—the bridge between self and other, the catalyst for growth, the seedbed of shared meaning. Through love, we become co-creators of a future shaped not merely by circumstance but by the intentional, collective pursuit of dreams.

Thus, relational love stands as a testament to the human spirit's capacity for renewal and transformation. It is an enduring legacy, passed across generations, sustained by those willing to nurture the delicate balance between stability and change. It is a living testament that love—when understood and practiced as a service—is the very engine of life itself.

Relational love operates like environmental carbon credits—each act of care generates "relational credits" that can be transferred, accumulated, and exchanged across social networks. Just as carbon credits incentivize positive environmental behavior, relational credits create feedback loops that reward emotional investment and vulnerability.

To deepen our understanding of love as a relational service, it is essential to explore how this active process manifests in everyday life. Love's expression is found not just in grand gestures or moments of passion but in the quiet, consistent commitments that weave the threads of connection tighter. It is present in the mundane routines of shared mornings, the patient listening when words falter, and the subtle adjustments made to honor one another's evolving needs.

These acts of attentiveness are far from trivial; they represent the deliberate labor of relational care. Such care demands an awareness that love is never static—it requires presence, intentionality, and the willingness to adapt. When love is practiced as a service, it becomes a continuous feedback loop where partners, friends, and communities co-create their shared reality, evolving together through open communication and mutual responsiveness.

This process mirrors the concept of relational intelligence—a capacity to perceive and respond sensitively to the changing emotional landscapes within interpersonal networks. Relational intelligence allows individuals to sense shifts in tone, mood, and energy, enabling timely recalibrations that prevent conflicts from hardening into permanent divides. It fosters empathy, not as a passive feeling but as an active skill, cultivated through ongoing practice and humility.

Moreover, relational love challenges traditional notions that reduce love to possession, dependency, or control. Instead, it frames love as freedom—the freedom to grow independently while remaining interdependently connected. It honors the autonomy of each individual within the relationship while recognizing that true flourishing arises from collaborative effort.

Healthy communities exhibit swarm intelligence similar to murmurations of starlings or colonies of social insects. Individual relational decisions create emergent collective behaviors that optimize for group survival and flourishing. No single relationship controls the overall pattern, yet the system responds to threats and opportunities with remarkable coordination and adaptability.

Like fungal networks that share nutrients between distant trees, relational love creates underground information and resource exchanges. The "wood wide web" demonstrates how seemingly separate entities maintain invisible supply chains of support—much like how emotional labor flows through social networks in ways that aren't immediately visible but are essential for collective thriving.

This shift carries profound implications for how we approach conflict and tension within relationships. Rather than viewing disagreements as threats, relational love invites us to perceive them as opportunities for growth—moments when the system flexes and tests its resilience. Navigating conflict with curiosity and respect transforms potential rupture into deeper understanding, reinforcing the bonds that hold the network intact.

In this light, love's risks are not reckless gambles but calculated investments. They require vulnerability and trust, acknowledging that openness invites both possibility and pain. Yet, it is precisely through this willingness to expose our authentic selves that relational love gains its transformative power. The courage to be seen wholly—flaws, fears, and all—is the very foundation upon which enduring connections are built.

In derivatives trading, some relationships involve emotional derivatives—complex instruments that derive value from underlying relational assets. A person might "short" vulnerability in one relationship while "going long" on emotional availability in another, managing risk across their relational portfolio.

These insights resonate not only at the personal level but also extend into collective and societal realms. Communities, organizations, and cultures thrive or falter based on their capacity to embody relational love at scale. When collective dreams align with shared values and mutual respect, they generate a powerful force for innovation, solidarity, and resilience.

This collective alignment demonstrates how individual relational choices aggregate into emergent social phenomena, much like natural systems that exhibit sophisticated coordination without centralized control. Conversely, societies that neglect relational love—prioritizing competition, isolation, or rigid hierarchies—risk fracturing under the weight of unmet human needs. This fragmentation breeds distrust, alienation, and ultimately instability. Recognizing love as a service thus calls for a radical reimagining of social structures that prioritize relational well-being as a core principle.

At its core, relational love invites a holistic perspective—one that honors the interconnectedness of emotional, psychological, and social dimensions. It encourages us to cultivate spaces where diverse voices can be heard and valued, fostering inclusion and belonging. Such environments become fertile grounds for collective dreaming and action, where innovation emerges not from isolated genius but from collaborative creativity.

To sustain this ecosystem, continuous learning and adaptation are essential. Just as ecosystems rely on biodiversity for resilience, relational networks depend on the richness of perspectives and experiences. This diversity requires us to challenge assumptions, confront biases, and embrace uncertainty as a necessary condition for growth.

Importantly, the metaphor of relational love as a service also illuminates the temporal dimension of connection. Unlike static commodities, relational bonds evolve over time, shaped by shared histories and future aspirations. The narrative we weave together— the stories, rituals, and symbols we create—imbues relationships with meaning and continuity.

This temporal flow demands that we honor both memory and possibility, balancing respect for what has been with openness to what can be. Such balancing acts require patience and grace, acknowledging that the path of relational love is rarely linear. Setbacks and regressions occur, but with commitment and care, these moments become part of the larger arc toward deeper connection.

Finally, this expanded understanding empowers us to redefine success in love and relationships. Success is no longer measured by permanence or predictability but by the capacity to sustain vitality, relevance, and growth. It is found in the dance between constancy and change, between holding on and letting go. This redefinition of success points toward a fundamental shift from extractive to regenerative models of emotional exchange, where the very act of loving creates abundance rather than scarcity.

Unlike extractive economic models that deplete resources, mature relational love operates on regenerative principles where emotional investment actually increases the total available emotional capital. Each act of authentic vulnerability and care creates surplus energy that compounds over time, generating exponential returns that benefit the entire relational ecosystem while leaving it more resilient than before.

In embracing love as a relational service, we accept an invitation to become co-authors of our shared destinies. We learn that love's true power lies not in possession or control but in service—service to the ongoing creation of connection, meaning, and life itself.

As we deepen our understanding of love as a dynamic, relational service—one rooted in continuous adaptation, mutual care, and shared purpose—it becomes clear that love does not exist in isolation. Its vitality depends not only on the intimate bonds we cultivate but also on the wider networks and exchanges that extend beyond personal relationships. The architecture of love, then, is inherently social and economic, embedded within systems of value, trust, and influence that transcend the private sphere.

This realization invites us to consider love from a new vantage point: as something that can be exchanged, leveraged, and transformed within broader social and economic contexts. If relational love is the foundational service sustaining human connection, tradeable love introduces the dimension where love's energy becomes a form of currency—imbued with symbolic meaning and exchanged in complex patterns of reciprocity.

Tradeable love challenges us to rethink the boundaries between emotion and economy, intimacy and transaction, generosity and negotiation. It asks how love's inherent generosity coexists with human tendencies toward exchange, and how the act of giving love can simultaneously be a form of investment, a source of power, or a catalyst for social capital.

By exploring love through this lens, we open new pathways to understand how affection, commitment, and care intersect with social structures and material realities. We begin to see how love flows through marketplaces of influence and meaning, shaping identities, forging alliances, and sustaining communities in ways both visible and subtle.

Today's technologies often align with this philosophy, like in the case of blockchain consensus mechanisms, where relational love functions as a distributed ledger where trust is built through consistent, verifiable actions across multiple validators (friends, family, community). Each interaction creates an immutable record that builds toward consensus about someone's relational "creditworthiness."

In medieval Islamic cities, the "muhtasib" served as market inspector with an extraordinary mandate: regulating not just weights and measures, but the emotional tenor of commercial relationships. These officials could fine merchants for failing to demonstrate proper hospitality, showing excessive greed, or creating atmospheres of distrust that damaged the marketplace's social fabric.

This created a radical model where emotional labor became legally mandated and professionally assessed. Merchants understood that their capacity for warmth and genuine care directly affected their commercial licenses. The muhtasib essentially created "emotional futures markets" where traders invested in cultivating relational skills, knowing these would yield returns through repeat customers and community standing.

The system institutionalized relational love as economic infrastructure, recognizing that markets collapse without underlying networks of trust. It made emotional intelligence a tradeable commodity with professional oversight, transforming commerce into a school for relational mastery where success depended on generating authentic human connection between strangers.

This historical example invites us to rethink love not merely as a private sentiment, but as a public force with economic and social weight. When care, trust, and emotional presence become prerequisites for doing business, love itself begins to circulate as a form of capital—something cultivated, expected, and exchanged. In this light, love becomes infrastructural, not ornamental. It is this expanded, systemic view that leads us into the next chapter.

As we transition into the chapter on Tradeable Love, we embark on a journey to uncover the ways love moves beyond private connection—how it becomes a vital, dynamic asset that can be cultivated, exchanged, and harnessed for collective benefit. This exploration will reveal the tensions and harmonies between love's intangible essence and its tangible manifestations within the networks we inhabit.

With this expanded perspective, we prepare to navigate the complex terrain where relational depth meets transactional possibility—where love serves not only as a service but also as a tradeable force shaping the fabric of human society.

Relational Love

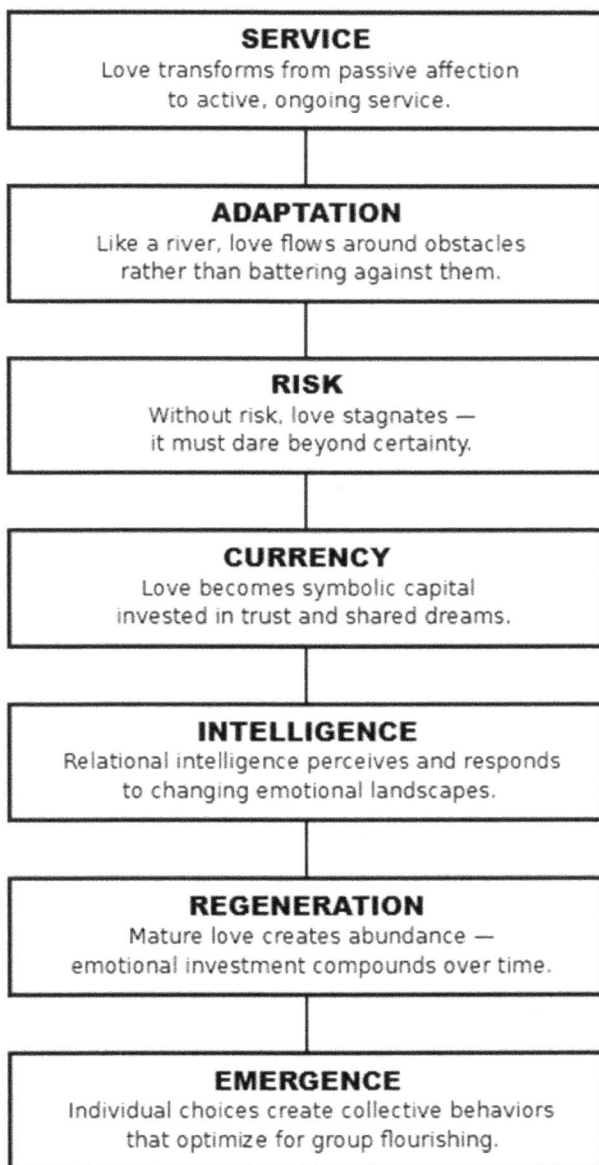

SERVICE
Love transforms from passive affection
to active, ongoing service.

ADAPTATION
Like a river, love flows around obstacles
rather than battering against them.

RISK
Without risk, love stagnates —
it must dare beyond certainty.

CURRENCY
Love becomes symbolic capital
invested in trust and shared dreams.

INTELLIGENCE
Relational intelligence perceives and responds
to changing emotional landscapes.

REGENERATION
Mature love creates abundance —
emotional investment compounds over time.

EMERGENCE
Individual choices create collective behaviors
that optimize for group flourishing.

Tradeable Love: Emotional Currency in Motion

In the grand theater of human existence, love unfolds as a complex dance—an intricate ballet woven from dreams, desires, and the silent threads of connection that bind us. Central to this dance is the role of money—a seemingly mundane instrument that, in truth, acts as the poetic brushstroke upon the canvas of our shared aspirations. Think of money not merely as paper or numbers but as an extension of our capacity to express love—a means to bridge individual worlds and transform fleeting passions into enduring realities.

Imagine a carnival bursting with emotions and hopes; each participant brings forth their own dreams—some seeking security, others craving recognition or creative fulfillment. Money becomes the silent orchestrator here: it weaves behind the scenes, facilitating exchanges that allow these dreams to flourish. When two hearts desire union or collaboration, they do so through this bridge—balancing perceived value against tangible worth. It safeguards fairness in transactions and ensures that intentions align with outcomes. Without it, connections risk becoming fragile whispers lost amid unspoken assumptions; with it, love can navigate complexities gracefully.

Yet we must understand that money's true power lies not in its possession but in its creation through acts of effort and creation. Every coin exchanged is a testament to contribution—an acknowledgment that one effort holds significance for another. This mutual recognition forms the foundation for genuine compromise: both parties agree on what is valuable based on shared effort rather than arbitrary claims or coercion. Money is thus a constructed symbol—a vessel embodying trust and honor within our social fabric.

Inside medieval guilds, the apprentice offered years of service, the journeyman contributed skill and loyalty, and the master provided wisdom and protection. Each stage demanded investment: the apprentice gave time and labor in exchange for knowledge and shelter, while the master invested patience and resources in return for dedication and eventual succession. This was not mere transaction but transformation—a sacred exchange where value flowed both ways, creating not just skilled artisans but entire communities built on mutual investment. Love circles operate on similar principles: we apprentice ourselves to understanding another's heart, journeying through seasons of giving and receiving, until we master the art of sustained connection.

In a world devoid of meaning attached to money—if exchange were driven solely by force or coercion—the very notion of voluntary compromise would dissolve into chaos. Instead, we rely on this collective agreement: a system where value is assigned through shared understanding and effort rather than exploitation or greed. When individuals contribute creatively within their unique economies—crafting goods or services—they reinforce this system's integrity. Their wallets become proof not just of wealth but of commitment; they symbolize an active participation in an ecosystem where love circles expand through mutual giving.

This principle underscores an essential moral truth: sustainable economies are rooted in creation—not theft nor plea bargaining—but in genuine contribution aligned with personal passions and collective aspirations. When love circles operate on such principles, they foster growth instead of stagnation; they propel us forward rather than trap us in inertia fueled by fear or complacency.

The Japanese art of kintsugi—mending broken pottery with gold—reveals a profound economic truth about love's durability. Rather than discarding cracked vessels, artisans transform breaks into beauty, using precious metal to highlight rather than hide the repair. The restored piece becomes more valuable than the original, not despite its history of fracture but because of how it chose to heal. This philosophy challenges our throwaway culture's approach to relationships: instead of discarding connections when they crack under pressure, we can choose to mend them with the gold of deeper understanding, creating bonds that are stronger and more beautiful for having been tested. The investment in repair often yields greater returns than the cost of replacement.

Consider now how these ideas influence your pursuit—for example—the quest for knighthood—the elevation within your community based upon honor and integrity. If relationships within your circle are transactional only at surface level—that is, if exchanges become mere commodities—you risk erosion of trust and diminished capacity for meaningful sacrifice. Conversely, when trade embodies genuine exchange driven by heartfelt contribution—the act itself becomes an expression of love—you build resilience against external uncertainties.

Money's role extends further: it provides certainty amid chaos—a buffer against known unknowns lurking at every turn—and offers pathways for creative expression without forcing compromises on your core values or personal sovereignty. It allows you to navigate unpredictable terrains while maintaining clarity about what truly matters: your integrity, your passion projects, your relationships.

No universal truth exists; instead, there are innumerable individual pursuits striving toward their own ideal versions—a mosaic where each piece reflects different dreams but all interconnect via mutual respect expressed through value exchanges akin to services rendered—not just goods bought or sold but expressions crafted from heartfelt intention.

Think about nature's garden: plants demand sunlight—and water—but even then, success depends on understanding each plant's unique needs and limitations—incompatible species may hinder growth if forced together artificially; similar logic applies when managing economies built upon diverse loves and talents. Value isn't self-produced—it must be acquired through intentional acts aligned with specific economic contexts—recognizing that one apple cannot substitute seamlessly for one chair unless appropriately valued within their respective worlds.

The dynamic exchange is fluid—not static—and money facilitates this flexibility by acting as a language capable of translating changing desires into actionable steps toward fulfillment—even as those desires evolve over time due to shifting circumstances—all while maintaining stability amidst volatility.

Within markets—from small barter systems among neighbors to vast stock exchanges—money functions as more than mere medium; it embodies collective hopes—and fears—and expectations about future actions—all rooted in mutual trust built through consistent contributions over time.

The ancient Silk Road understood what modern markets often forget—that value emerges not from individual accumulation but from the patient cultivation of trust across vast distances and cultural divides. A Chinese silk merchant might never meet the Roman patrician who eventually wore his fabric, yet their transaction was made possible by a chain of relationships stretching across continents: the caravan leader who vouched for quality, the Persian middleman who bridged languages, the Byzantine banker who guaranteed payment. Each link in this chain invested not just goods but reputation, creating a network where a promise made in Chang'an held weight in Constantinople. This same principle governs lasting love: we build value not through grand gestures alone but through countless small acts of reliability that compound across time, creating trust networks that can bear the weight of our deepest vulnerabilities.

However—and here lies the paradox—we often fall prey to speculation driven by irrational fears concerning unknown unknowns—the unseen forces shaping markets beyond our immediate perception—which leads us astray into inertia: paralysis born out of anxiety rather than clarity.

This brings us back again—to fundamental principles rooted deep inside our social DNA—to cooperation based upon equitable compromise rather than dominance rooted solely in power dynamics.

Game theory offers insight here via Nash equilibrium—a state where no individual gains by unilaterally changing their choice because all parties have found satisfactory balances between supply and demand. Such equilibria emerge after trial-and-error processes—as industries find acceptable prices for interchangeable products like soft drinks—they mirror interpersonal negotiations within love circles too. Your acceptance or rejection of value propositions reflects alignment or misalignment with community desires.

Without money—as without language—you'd struggle profoundly—to translate inner visions into outer realities—to manifest dreams into tangible expressions. Money enables you not just individually but collectively—to intersect disparate aspirations—from growing apples to crafting chairs—as part of larger ecosystems fueled by ongoing transactions grounded in mutual respect.

It permits growth without sacrificing authenticity—in fact—it amplifies it because each act carries weight beyond mere materiality—it embodies commitment—not just monetary wealth but emotional richness too.

When you pursue wealth purely for its own sake—you risk losing sight of what truly matters—for wealth divorced from purpose breeds stagnation—inertia—it turns lovers into spectators rather than participants-in-creation.

Instead focus on expressing love's essence—in acts aimed at enriching others' lives: whether planting orchards, building furniture, tending lawns, or simply offering kindness— you contribute creatively when guided by authentic intent—and such contributions forge resilient love circles capable even amidst uncertainty.

Money then becomes less an end—a symbol manipulated by external forces—and more a facilitator—a partner guiding you along your noble journey toward higher honor—not merely accumulating possessions but elevating relationships rooted deeply in shared purpose.

In essence: To trade means more than exchanging objects; it's exchanging meanings, it's translating inner visions into outer realities, it's fostering bonds across diverse worlds, all enabled seamlessly when monetary systems align with authentic efforts— when revenue flows from real passion— and when every transaction echoes true connection instead of merely superficial gain.

Remember—that true wealth isn't measured solely by figures— but by depth: the depth invested in nurturing loved ones, the breadth reached through expanding horizons, and the richness beneath each act—that which makes life worth living: the ability to give freely without losing oneself—in other words: chase not after wealth itself; chase after expressing your unique brand of love—for therein lies infinite richness beyond measure.

Even in the tender moments of unspoken affection or a glance passed between lovers, there exists a quiet ledger: a history of what has been given, received, and understood. The tokens we offer—be they words, gestures, or finely wrapped boxes—carry encoded signals of worth. These are not just sentimental acts but economic ones, expressions of investment into a shared future.

The old idea that love should be "priceless" often ignores the truth that everything we do to sustain it is, in some way, a cost: of energy, of presence, of what else we could be doing instead. And that cost, far from tainting the purity of love, is what makes it real. We don't devalue a sculpture because it took thousands of hours to carve; the effort becomes part of its beauty. So too in love: the effort to understand another's needs, to contribute to their joy, is its own art form—paid for not in coins, but in focused attention, in sacrifices made freely, in projects built together.

And yet, effort without structure falters. It is not enough to want; one must also navigate. And money—though often portrayed as the enemy of love—is a compass when used wisely. It shows us how much we are willing to bend, to budget, to create in the name of sustaining something larger than ourselves. When two individuals sit at the table and plan a life, they engage not just in emotional labor but economic planning—trading dreams, measuring feasibility, outlining shared aspirations in a language both understand.

The Dutch flower auctions of Aalsmeer reveal a profound truth about timing and value in relationships. Here, in the world's largest flower market, buyers must make split-second decisions as prices tick downward—waiting too long means losing the prize entirely, bidding too early means overpaying for what might have been obtained more cheaply. Yet the most successful buyers are not those who chase every bloom, but those who know precisely what they seek and what they're willing to invest. They study seasonal patterns, understand quality markers, and develop relationships with growers who share their commitment to excellence. When two people sit down to plan their shared future, they engage in a similar delicate calibration—learning to recognize when opportunity presents itself, understanding the true cost of what they desire, and developing the patience to wait for alignment between dreams and reality. The wisdom lies not in hesitation or haste, but in preparation meeting possibility.

It is here, in these shared blueprints, that love becomes tradeable not because it is cheap, but because it is substantial. It has become real enough to manage. Like a business plan built from joy, a relationship grows through consistency, contribution, and sometimes compromise. We often resist this framing because we mistake "trade" for transactionalism, but the truth is: all lasting love is transactional. Not cold or calculating, but reciprocal, dynamic, and evolving.

The Aboriginal concept of gift economy reveals another dimension of tradeable love: the understanding that true wealth circulates rather than accumulates. In these societies, status came not from what you owned but from what you could give away, creating spiraling networks of reciprocity that bound communities together across generations. A hunter who shared his catch earned not just gratitude but a place in an invisible web of mutual support that would sustain him through future hardships. This wisdom translates beautifully to intimate relationships: the more we give authentically, the more we create networks of care that return to us in unexpected ways. The gift economy teaches us that love's value increases when shared rather than hoarded, multiplying through generous circulation rather than diminishing through careful conservation.

A hug, a compliment, a listening ear—each is a currency in the economy of affection. When these are given with sincerity and returned in kind, a surplus of trust is built. But when one party overextends without return, emotional inflation takes hold: the words grow hollow, the gestures lose weight, and the structure buckles. There is no shame in keeping emotional books balanced. In fact, it is only by acknowledging these invisible exchanges that true generosity can flourish—generosity that is not performative, but honest, measured, and resilient.

The ancient Romans understood this delicate balance intimately. When a bride's family delivered a dowry, it was not merely a payment but a statement of commitment—often paid in careful installments over three years, with great honor accorded to those who could offer the full amount at once. This wasn't about purchasing love but about demonstrating serious intent, providing security, and establishing a foundation for shared prosperity. The dowry served as both gift and investment, a tangible manifestation of families weaving their futures together. In our modern love circles, we offer our own forms of dowry—not in coins but in consistency, not in property but in presence, not in goods but in the goods of our character steadily revealed over time.

There's an undeniable tension between idealized love and practical reality. Culture may teach us to expect love to flourish "despite everything"—without limits, regardless of conditions. But in truth, the most enduring connections are the ones that acknowledge boundaries and work within them. Partners who build something sustainable don't ignore the ledger; they co-author it, ensuring both hearts and wallets are tended with care.

And it is not merely romantic love that thrives in this economy of meaning. Friendship too, and family, and mentorship—all these are forms of tradeable love, where the value exchanged is not quantifiable in dollars, but is felt in the depth of shared experiences. Consider the friend who helps you move, or the sibling who lends an ear at midnight. These are not acts of charity—they are deposits into a shared account of loyalty and support, to be drawn upon when tides shift.

Some may recoil at this notion, fearful it reduces love to business, to balance sheets. But that critique misses the core insight: tradeable love increases when it is seen as worth managing. We do not say that tending a garden reduces its beauty; rather, we admire the patience and dedication behind every bloom. Love, like soil, must be enriched, watered, and rotated. Money merely gives us one more tool in our hands—a way to turn that labor into action, to back intent with logistics, to fertilize connection with stability.

Even in art, we see this fusion of emotion and economy. A painter sells a canvas, not to cheapen their vision, but to fund more paint, more time, more work. And what is a relationship, if not a living artwork? A dance of investment and return. Two people deciding, again and again, that the labor of building together is worth the effort—that what they're creating is too precious to leave to chance alone.

This doesn't mean love should always be monetized—but it can be materialized. It can take the shape of a home paid for together, a vacation saved for patiently, a gift that carries more than market value—it carries story. To dismiss the economic side of love is to ignore half its language. To honor it is to build sturdier bridges between hope and fulfillment.

And in moments of hardship, it is often the economic scaffolding that keeps the emotional edifice from collapsing. When storms arrive—illness, unemployment, grief—it is not only love that sustains, but the reserves built from shared contribution. The emergency fund, the habits of giving and receiving, the unspoken contracts reinforced over years—all these transform crises into continuity. Here, money is not just helpful—it is humane.

Still, there is danger in imbalance. When one uses money to dominate, to dictate, to replace emotional presence with financial offerings, the structure tilts. Tradeable love only works when both sides remain equal partners—when the trade is mutual, not manipulative. The moment money becomes a means of control, it ceases to be love's ally and becomes its adversary.

But if we hold fast to the principle of mutual uplift—if we trade not for control, but for cooperation—then love is not compromised by money; it is empowered. You can build altars with your earnings. You can turn paychecks into poetry, rent into sanctuary, meals into memories. And in doing so, you prove that what you value is not just having, but holding—holding space, holding time, holding one another.

Even solitude finds resonance here. The single parent budgeting for their child's future. The artist working two jobs to afford the studio. The elder giving away their savings to a cause they believe in. These are acts of tradeable love too—where money becomes a stand-in for presence, a vessel for care, a tangible echo of what the heart holds dear.

It's not wealth that gives love its meaning—but the willingness to use whatever you have in service of someone else's thriving. That could be a coin, a word, an hour, a hand. That could be giving up comfort for someone else's peace. In these exchanges—measured or not—value emerges, not as price, but as purpose.

Even in the most intimate spaces, money reveals itself not as an intruder but as a mirror—a quiet reflection of how we prioritize, honor, and invest in each other. It does not replace emotion; it clarifies it. It shows up in the small decisions: who pays for dinner, who takes time off work to care for a sick partner, who shoulders the rent when dreams falter. Each of these choices becomes a thread in the tapestry of relational value—not because of the monetary amount but because of the energy and intention behind it.

This isn't to say love should be transactional in the cold, calculating sense. Rather, it acknowledges that love—when expressed through daily life—inevitably intersects with systems of value. The gift given, the time taken, the support extended—all carry weight in both emotional and economic terms. To deny this is to risk misalignment between what is felt and what is expressed. We do not just feel love—we enact it. And money becomes one of its most common, though not always conscious, enactments.

It is in this enactment that love becomes visible—not just in the candlelit moments, but in the planning of futures, the pooling of resources, and the brave decisions to invest in another's potential. Think of the parent who sacrifices personal luxuries to fund a child's education—not for ROI in the financial sense, but for an emotional return: witnessing a dream unfold. That transaction, while seemingly economic, is rich with love, commitment, and belief. The money spent is not simply gone—it is transformed into opportunity, hope, and continuity.

Similarly, partners in love often navigate shared finances not merely to manage bills but to co-author a life. What they buy, save for, or forego reflects their values and priorities. A home isn't just a shelter; it's a symbol of stability. A vacation isn't merely a trip—it's a reprieve carved out for togetherness. Even the decisions to budget or splurge tell stories: of restraint, desire, vision, or sacrifice. When both parties bring conscious awareness to this narrative, the financial becomes an act of co-creation rather than contention.

Of course, danger lurks when these exchanges are unbalanced—when one gives and the other only takes. In such cases, money reveals ruptures that emotion alone might conceal. It highlights mismatches in effort, appreciation, or reciprocity. And so, rather than corrupting love, it may clarify whether love is truly mutual. This clarification can be painful, but it is necessary. For love, to endure, must be rooted not only in passion but in fairness.

We live in a world where the commodification of everything often threatens to blur the sacred lines. Weddings become industries, gestures become expectations, and social media turns affection into performance. But even within this noise, authenticity remains possible—if we remember that money itself is neutral. It is the motive and the context that color it. A $10 bill can be a bribe or a blessing. A diamond ring can be a hollow status symbol or a deeply meaningful commitment. The object doesn't speak; we do, through it.

In that sense, tradeable love asks us not to detach from money, but to imbue it with meaning. To use it intentionally. To ask, not "how much?" but "to what end?" When you buy a gift for your partner, it's not about the price tag but the attention behind the gesture. When you fund a dream with your earnings, you're not buying success—you're watering a seed of purpose. And when you support someone financially during their time of need, you're not paying them—you're standing with them.

These decisions form the architecture of trust. They say, "I see you; I believe in you; I'm invested in your well-being." In that way, money becomes an instrument of love's longevity—not because love needs financing, but because life does. And love, when integrated into life, must learn the language of real-world effort.

Yet the most transcendent aspect of tradeable love lies in its circular nature. When you contribute meaningfully to someone's life—whether through labor, money, or time—you enrich both them and yourself. Their growth, joy, and success reverberate back to you. This is why generosity doesn't deplete; it multiplies. When done from the heart, giving is not subtraction—it is alchemy. Something unseen becomes manifest. A dream becomes possible. A bond deepens.

But herein lies the paradox: for love to remain love, giving must be offered freely, not demanded. Tradeable love is not transactional love. It's not tit-for-tat. Rather, it's love that recognizes we all have limited resources—of time, energy, money—and choosing to invest those in someone is a profound act of prioritization. It says, "You matter more than my other options." That is no small statement.

Over time, tradeable love builds a record—not of debts or IOUs, but of evidence. Evidence that both parties are building something greater than themselves. A home, a family, a vision. This shared account of love isn't tallied in bank statements but in memories, in milestones, in mutual sacrifices that paved the way forward. Love becomes a currency that accrues in meaning—not in accumulation but in flow.

This kind of economy resists greed and celebrates sufficiency. It resists exploitation and honors reciprocity. And perhaps most importantly, it resists apathy. It demands awareness—of the impact of your actions, of the needs of your partner, of the larger social systems that affect you both. It invites you to be intentional in how you love, how you earn, how you give, and how you receive.

When practiced well, tradeable love becomes a kind of invisible contract—not enforced by law but by honor. A mutual agreement to show up, to contribute, to communicate, and to grow together. Not every couple signs this contract consciously. Many fall into patterns shaped by upbringing, culture, or trauma. But even then, the contract exists—sometimes in silence, sometimes in struggle, sometimes in renewal.

And if the contract is breached—through betrayal, neglect, or indifference—the rupture is felt not just emotionally but existentially. Because when someone has entrusted you with their resources, their time, their attention—you hold a part of their life. To misuse that is to misuse them. Thus, tradeable love carries with it a sacred responsibility: to honor the invisible threads binding intention to expression, effort to outcome, soul to system.

In the end, money is not the root of all evil. Misalignment is. Disconnection is. Lovelessness is. Money is simply a tool—like language, like architecture, like music. In the hands of the fearful, it builds cages. In the hands of the loving, it builds bridges.

So let it build. Let it create. Let it nourish. Trade not just your goods but your care, your time, your creative output. Let your economy be full of soul, not scarcity. Let your currency carry the signature of your heart. For in doing so, you don't just build wealth—you build the conditions for possibility.

Because tradeable love is not the destination; it is the foundation. It establishes trust, co-ownership, shared investment. And from that shared ground, we begin to dream.

Love, when sustained through intentional giving and receiving, starts to lift its gaze. It stops asking, "What do we have now?" and begins to wonder, "What could we build next?" This is where love evolves into vision—not a fleeting fantasy, but a shared commitment to futures still unseen.

When two people dream together, they plant seeds in the soil of today with the eyes of tomorrow. They become co-architects of realities that don't yet exist. Just as venture capital backs unproven ideas with belief and boldness, visionary love invests in the intangible: potential, purpose, transformation.

Tradeable love sustains the present. Visionary love dares to transform it.

And so, let us move forward—toward love not just as value exchanged, but as foresight embodied. Toward love as the act of building futures from the raw materials of trust. Toward a love that sees the world not only as it is, but as it could be—and begins.

Tradeable Love

EXPRESSION
Love is made visible through action,
translating emotion into contribution.

EXCHANGE
Value is created when meaning and effort
are recognized and reciprocated.

EFFORT
Shared labor builds shared meaning—
investment gives love its substance.

TRUST
Sustained connection depends on reliability,
built over time through consistent exchange.

REPAIR
Breakdowns are opportunities to deepen bonds
when met with care, humility, and intention.

CIRCULATION
Love gains power through flow—
what is shared multiplies in return.

MATERIALIZATION
Resources embody care when aligned with values—
love becomes tangible through mindful provision.

Visionary Love: Dreaming the Future

Love, in its most exalted form, does not ask for permission to exist. It emerges—often unbidden—from the secret places of the soul, from longing spaces too deep for language and too ancient for reason. It is not content to merely survive in the mundane; it seeks always to become. And so, love reveals itself as the primordial architect of possibility. It conjures futures not yet born and dares the heart to move before the path is clear. One might think of it as a whisper in the dark, coaxing us forward into spaces unknown—not with certainty, but with the warmth of trust. This is not the fragile love that flinches in the face of doubt, but the enduring, radiant force that binds vision to reality, and intention to transformation. It is the light in the eyes of the one who dreams not only for themselves, but for a world that aches for meaning.

In the quiet solitude of thought, a single dream is conceived. It trembles with newness, like a flame kindled beneath a sleeping sky. The dream itself is small at first—barely formed, shapeless, an impulse of yearning. But even this glimmer bears the secret of worlds. For the dream is the seed, and the imagination is the soil. And when nurtured by belief, the dream swells into vision—a vivid, magnetic future that dares the dreamer to act. What begins as a fragile idea grows teeth and wings and pulse; it acquires gravity. It begins to call others toward it. The visionary is not merely one who sees—but one who believes with such intensity that others begin to see too.

To love with vision is to live with a profound responsibility. It is not enough to admire the stars; one must become a builder of constellations. Love—true, visionary love—is the force that invites the dream to take form in the world. It is not content with private longing. It wants to be shared, to become language and gesture and movement. It becomes kindness offered in silence, the hand extended when none is watching, the decision to create beauty even in a collapsing world. And it becomes action. For without action, vision remains an exquisite illusion—poetic, yes, but ultimately hollow. Love, when visionary, demands that we build what we see, and that we become what we believe is possible.

The ancient Kula ring of the Trobriand Islands was a ceremonial exchange that spanned eighteen island communities, where precious shells traveled vast oceanic distances not for their material worth, but as vessels of relationship itself. Participants traveled incredible distances in order to exchange Kula valuables that served as markers of status, yet the true currency was never the shells, but the bonds they wove between strangers across the sea. So too does visionary love create its own Kula ring—a sacred circulation where acts of care, moments of witness, and gestures of faith pass from heart to heart, accumulating not wealth but connection. The gift multiplies in the giving, returning transformed, carrying with it the essence of every soul it has touched.

This love does not shield us from hardship; it prepares us for it. It insists upon growth. It uses suffering as a chisel, reshaping us not into perfection, but into authenticity. It embraces the paradox that from brokenness may arise the most indestructible form of hope. Visionary love is not born from comfort; it is born from confrontation—confrontation with our fears, with the inertia of what has always been, with the seductive weight of resignation. It says: You are more than what the world has told you. You are more than even you can see. And so, it demands that we reach inward with honesty, and outward with bravery.

Yet in this reaching, the path is not always clear. The visionary walks a road that is often invisible to the many, lit only by the inner fire that refuses to go out. There are nights when the dream seems too fragile to hold, when silence mocks the effort and progress feels like a distant myth. But still, the heart continues. Because something in us knows that to give up the vision is to abandon not only the dream, but the soul of the dreamer. That is the secret gift of love— it lends us the strength to persist even when the world gives us no reason. It wraps itself around the wounded places and says: This too shall shape the story.

In the courts of medieval Languedoc, Eleanor was known for her patronage of troubadours and poets, who celebrated courtly love through their writings—a peculiar economy where love itself became both currency and commodity. The troubadour's song was payment for the patron's protection, yet the patron's gold was less valuable than the immortality offered by verse. Here was love made tradeable not through diminishment, but through multiplication— each ballad a promissory note that the beloved's essence would outlive empires. The true tender was not coin but recognition: the acknowledgment that to love with vision requires witnesses, that the dreamer needs the listener as much as the listener needs the dream.

What begins as an individual vision becomes a force that seeks connection. Visionary love is never self-contained. It yearns to multiply, to be mirrored in others, to inspire and ignite. In its purest state, it is generative—it creates room for others to dream too. It makes the invisible visible, not through assertion but invitation. It does not demand allegiance; it awakens resonance. It speaks in the language of the soul and is heard in the silent recognition of shared humanity. Love such as this refuses to dominate. It liberates. It leads by listening, and governs by grace.

And when this love is shared, it becomes a movement. Two visions aligned can bend the trajectory of time. Ten can shift a culture. A thousand, with shared heart and clarity of purpose, can reshape history. But here lies the sacred caution: vision must never become weapon. Even the most luminous ideals can be twisted into instruments of control if wielded without humility. That is the shadow side of vision—when it forgets the dignity of difference. True visionary love does not seek obedience. It seeks awakening. And it leaves room, always, for the unknown—the yet-to-be-discovered truths that live in others.

Children remind us of this. They carry within them uncarved futures—imagination unburdened by precedent. To love a child with vision is not to shape them in our image, but to become custodians of their emerging light. It is to honor their questions more than our answers. It is to stand in awe of what may yet become. Visionary love toward the young means resisting the urge to direct, and instead choosing to uplift—to protect the wildness of their dreaming until they are ready to name it for themselves. They teach us again that the future is not inherited, but imagined.

Children inhabit an instinctive gift economy, their love flowing without ledger or expectation of return. They offer dandelions as treasure, crayon drawings as masterpieces, sticky-fingered hugs as the highest form of wealth. In their world, attention is the rarest currency—more precious than gold because it cannot be manufactured, only given. They understand what we forget: that the economy of the heart operates on abundance, not scarcity. Every moment of wonder shared doubles rather than divides. Every story told becomes a legacy, every game played becomes a memory that compounds interest across generations. They remind us that in the truest market of meaning, we are all venture capitalists, investing in futures we cannot fully foresee.

And perhaps this is the call of visionary love: to imagine better not only for ourselves, but for all who will come after. To build, knowing we may not see the finished work. To act with courage rooted not in outcome, but in alignment. It is the kind of love that sits beside despair and does not flinch. The kind that makes art in ruins. That sings into silence. That keeps showing up even when no one is listening. Because it knows: everything of value begins this way.

In the presence of visionary love, even the most fractured spirits begin to mend. It speaks to the parts of us that have longed to be seen, the desires we've silenced, and the futures we've dared not articulate aloud. It offers not just comfort, but a mirror—showing us who we are becoming, not just who we've been. This love compels us to look ahead with reverence and responsibility, knowing that every choice we make today carves the path for those who will follow. It teaches us that to love with vision is to accept stewardship of something greater than the self, something vast and unfinished that calls forth our best efforts.

And yet, visionary love is not grandiose. It thrives in subtlety— in the quiet persistence of someone who plants trees they'll never sit under, or the teacher who ignites a flame in a child's eyes without needing credit for the fire. It is the artist sketching futures on blank walls, the community builder seeing harmony in a fractured neighborhood, the parent dreaming of a kinder world for their child. Visionary love is humble in its approach but radical in its consequences. It doesn't rush or demand recognition—it simply is, enduring and powerful, like the roots beneath an ancient tree that hold everything steady even in the storm.

In the scriptoriums of medieval monasteries, monks labored for decades illuminating manuscripts they would never see completed, each generation inheriting the work of the last and bequeathing it to the next. Their economy of devotion operated on temporal arbitrage—investing present toil for future revelation, trading immediate gratification for eternal significance. These scribes understood that some forms of love mature only across centuries, that certain visions require multiple lifetimes to fully capitalize. Their gold was not held in coffers but pressed into parchment, their wealth measured not in accumulation but in transmission. They created an economy where knowledge itself became sacred currency, where each carefully rendered letter was both prayer and payment toward a future they would never see but helped to guarantee.

But for such love to endure, it must be replenished. That is the second great truth of visionary love: it cannot flow forever from a vessel left empty. Self-love, then, is not a luxury—it is a necessity. When we forget to tend to the wellspring within, we risk turning our visions brittle, driven by obligation rather than inspiration. Those who love with vision know when to pause, to reflect, to rest—not out of indulgence, but out of wisdom. They understand that clarity comes from stillness as much as from striving, that the fire of purpose burns brighter when it is fed, not forced.

Nature herself operates on the economics of visionary love— forests investing carbon in soil they will never directly utilize, rivers carrying nutrients to deltas they will never see flower. The mycelial networks beneath our feet trade information and resources in an underground economy older than commerce, where the gift of glucose flows freely between species in exchange for minerals and messages. Trees recognize their offspring and send them sustenance through root systems that operate on principles of mutual aid rather than competition. This is the biomimicry of visionary love: understanding that true wealth circulates, that hoarding breaks the very networks that create abundance, that the forest's economy of care makes every individual tree more resilient than any could be in isolation.

The visionary lovers walk a paradoxical path—they carry light for others, but they must also shield their own flame. They believe in possibility even when the world insists on limitation. They are dreamers who act, not with naivety, but with unrelenting hope. Their love is not bound by outcome, but by intention—by the promise to show up again and again, no matter the result. And in doing so, they create something rare: a legacy that lives beyond them, woven into the lives they've touched and the futures they've dared to shape.

This love calls forth courage—not the loud, brash kind, but the kind that remains when no one is watching. It's the courage to keep building when others mock your blueprints, to keep dreaming when every statistic says you shouldn't. It is the courage to speak with tenderness in a world armored by cynicism, to extend trust even after betrayal, to show mercy where justice alone would be easier.

Visionary love is not weak. It is, perhaps, the most resilient force on Earth.

And as it expands, it invites others to do the same—to believe, to hope, to act. Like music passed ear to ear across time, visionary love moves through culture, through lineage, through story. It is not static; it evolves with us. It finds new expressions in every age—in revolutions, in resistance, in science and song and innovation. What once began as a quiet longing in one heart can become a movement that changes the fate of millions. That is the alchemy of love guided by vision: it multiplies.

When we choose to love this way—not merely to feel but to embody a greater purpose—we join a lineage of change makers. We become the bridge between what is and what could be. We stop waiting for better days to arrive and begin forging them ourselves. And in doing so, we remind others of their own capacity to dream, to create, to transform. Love spreads not by decree but by example. It inspires, not instructs. It breathes possibility into the air, making space for others to imagine lives they've yet to live.

This is why visionary love is never satisfied with stagnation. It listens deeply but does not accept resignation. It acknowledges pain but seeks healing. It sees clearly what is wrong and still chooses to believe in what could be made right. It is not blind—it is luminous, illuminating the path not just for those who walk it now, but for all who will walk it later. To love this way is to live as a lighthouse, not a judge; a beacon, not a gatekeeper. You guide by shining, not by shouting.

In a world so often seduced by short-term gain and instant gratification, visionary love is an act of rebellion. It asks us to invest in what may not yield results tomorrow but will ripple through decades. It is, in the truest sense, generational. And because of that, it requires both patience and faith. You must learn to plant gardens you may never see bloom. You must be willing to love not for applause, but for alignment—with your values, with your vision, with your deepest truth.

And though this journey may sometimes feel lonely, you are never alone. The path of visionary love is walked by many—quiet heroes whose names you may never know, souls who persist behind the scenes, building, dreaming, tending to the future. You are part of that fellowship now. Every time you choose integrity over ease, courage over comfort, generosity over gain—you echo their steps. And one day, someone else will echo yours.

This is how the world changes. Not always through revolution, but through reverence. Through love that looks far ahead and still acts here, now—with purpose, with clarity, with heart. Visionary love is not a destination, but a way of being. A discipline. A devotion. A promise you make to tomorrow by how you live today.

You are the keeper of this flame. Let it burn. Let it guide. Let it grow.

Successful organizations mirror this delicate balance—they hold onto core principles while adapting strategies to meet changing circumstances without sacrificing the essence—that intangible yet vital spark that keeps their mission alive across generations.

This capacity for adaptation hinges on trust—the bedrock upon which visionary pursuits stand firm amidst shifting landscapes—and on gratitude—the recognition that past efforts have laid foundations for future growth rather than dead ends buried beneath complacency.

Visionary love thus becomes an art: weaving dreams so compelling they stir hearts globally—transforming personal aspirations into collective movements capable not only of change but of lasting impact.

Leonardo da Vinci epitomized such visionary devotion—his relentless pursuit across disciplines exemplifies how unwavering passion, coupled with imaginative foresight, gives birth to innovations no single mind could conceive alone—from his sketches dreaming up flying machines to anatomical studies revealing unseen marvels.

Nelson Mandela similarly embodies visionary love: committed unwaveringly amid adversity, his dedication reshaped South Africa's destiny through forgiveness inspired by profound belief in human potential despite oppression.

When long-held beliefs align closely with what individuals genuinely care about most—their deepest values—they forge irreplaceable bonds driving persistent effort toward shared goals even amidst failures.

Yet challenges remain universal: obstacles confront all who seek transformation—including moments when clarity dims under pressure or distractions threaten focus—but true lovers of vision confront these hurdles head-on because their commitment isn't superficial nor blind; it perceives beneath surface flaws—to see potential even within imperfections—and strives relentlessly toward realization.

Love endowed with such foresight elevates beyond fleeting emotion—it transforms itself into devotion—a sacred pledge toward creating something greater than oneself. The kindling fire fueling generations long after initial sparks fade away—to leave behind ripples shaping tomorrow's world.

In essence, visionary love merges deep affection with expansive imagination—a force capable both of attractively inspiring others and of uniting diverse souls under common banners rooted in noble ideals. Its power lies not merely in dreaming but in actively manifesting those dreams through consistent action built upon trust and integrity.

Leonardo dared imagine flight before its reality; Mandela dreamed justice before its dawn. These examples remind us: if you see beyond what appears visible now—if you nurture your inner fire until it blazes bright—you become both architect and guardian of transformative change.

Let it grow in the way you speak, in the way you listen. Let it shape your presence in rooms where people feel unseen. Let it fill the spaces where fear has silenced boldness. Visionary love is not always loud, but it is always present. Even in your smallest decisions, it can live—when you choose honesty over convenience, when you protect someone's dignity instead of tearing them down, when you forgive even when no one asks you to.

And when you falter—and you will—let that too be part of love's vision. Let your missteps become teachers. Visionary love doesn't require perfection; it only asks for intention. It welcomes growth, adaptation, and humility. It understands that transformation is not a single act, but a series of small, faithful turns toward the person you're becoming. Every time you realign with your values after drifting, you strengthen the very love you aim to give.

In this way, visionary love becomes a spiritual discipline. Not just a feeling, but a choice you renew each day. It challenges the ego and nurtures the soul. It demands responsibility but gives freedom in return. It expands your view of self—not as isolated, but as part of a vast, interconnected future. With this awareness, your life becomes a vessel—not only for what you need, but for what you are called to contribute.

The world may never thank you. Visionary love is not transactional. It does not seek validation, only alignment with what is just and true. And still, this love rewards you in ways the world cannot. It gives you integrity as your compass, clarity as your companion, and peace as your home. You no longer chase fulfillment—you become it.

When you love with vision, your life begins to echo beyond you. Your choices ripple into other lives, other times. Maybe it's the child who grows up safe because you created a space where safety was sacred. Maybe it's the stranger who remembers your kindness when deciding how they'll treat someone else. Maybe it's the future leader who reads your words, sees your art, hears your truth, and decides they too can believe in more.

This is the invisible architecture of change: love that lives on not in monuments, but in motion. In what we pass forward, in what we preserve, in what we protect. Visionary love is legacy—not carved in stone, but etched into the lives we touch. It cannot be undone, only expanded.

So, protect your vision. Guard your heart not with walls, but with wisdom. Surround yourself with people who nourish your purpose. Rest when needed. Grieve when you must. But never lose the thread of who you are and what you love for. Keep coming back to it, even in the quiet. Especially in the quiet.

Because in the end, this kind of love isn't just a gift you give to the world—it's the world you build by how you love. And it starts with you.

But visionary love, as bold and expansive as it is, cannot sustain itself on inspiration alone. Dreams need structure. Passion needs rhythm. Without the quiet constancy of care, even the brightest vision fades.

To give love shape, we must return to it daily—not just in grand moments, but in the smallest repetitions. In gestures so subtle they could be overlooked, yet powerful enough to shift the soul. This is where love deepens, where it matures—not through drama, but through devotion.

It is in the repeated offering of presence. The way your hands fold the same blanket each night. The way your voice softens during forgiveness. The way you choose to stay, to listen, to tend—even when no one is watching. These are not just habits; they are sacred practices. Devotional love transforms the ordinary into the holy. It teaches us that every act of care is a prayer, every moment of intention a kind of worship.

So, as we leave the realm of vision, we now step into the sanctuary of devotion. Here, love becomes more than a force—it becomes a ritual. An offering. A way of being.

Visionary Love

EMERGENCE
Love arises from the soul's depth,
not for permission, but to become.

IMAGINATION
A dream kindles vision,
gaining gravity and calling others forward.

RESPONSIBILITY
To love with vision is to build,
to act, to transform vision into form.

CIRCULATION
Visionary love flows and multiplies,
connecting hearts through shared care.

RESILIENCE
Visionary love endures through hardship,
growing stronger through challenge and hope.

GENERATIVITY
It awakens possibility in others,
mirroring vision to inspire new dreams.

LEGACY
It echoes beyond the individual,
transforming moments into movements.

Devotional Love: Rituals and Repetition

Devotional love holds a unique position, one that far surpasses the fleeting whims and transient pleasures so often mistaken for affection. It is an investment not of capital or commodities but of time, trust, and unwavering faith, yielding dividends that accrue steadily across the span of a lifetime. Much like prudent financial planning, this form of love is not about rapid gains or speculative risks; rather, it calls for patience, consistent effort, and an understanding that the true value lies not in immediate gratification but in enduring growth.

Imagine love as a complex market, a realm where emotions act as currency and every interaction represents a transaction. In such a marketplace, many ventures can seem enticing—flashy, promising quick returns but ultimately lacking the foundation to sustain themselves. Devotional love, by contrast, is akin to a blue-chip stock or a carefully selected bond—secure and dependable, weathering the storms and recessions that inevitably strike. It requires that we allocate our emotional resources wisely, much like an investor who scrutinizes the stability and potential of their assets. This isn't a reckless plunge into volatile waters but a deliberate, thoughtful commitment to something that appreciates steadily over time.

While day traders chase volatile profits that can vanish overnight, pension fund managers think in decades, understanding that consistent, patient contributions yield the security that sustains a lifetime.

At the heart of this process is the idea of "emotional capital," a reservoir built through small, intentional acts that might appear insignificant in isolation but compound exponentially. Much like the principle of compound interest that transforms modest deposits into considerable wealth, devotional love thrives on the daily gestures of kindness and patience. A gentle word, a moment of understanding during tension, a willingness to forgive—each deposits value into the shared account of the relationship. Over days, months, and years, these accumulated acts form a deep well of affection and security, fortifying the bond against life's inevitable upheavals.

Consider Manhattan's High Line transformation—a 20-year vision that converted abandoned railway into prime real estate, increasing surrounding property values 1000%. Devotional love undertakes similar long-term development: seeing potential in emotional wastelands, investing consistent care until neglected areas of intimacy become the relationship's most treasured spaces. What appears worthless—a partner's stubborn quirks, recurring disagreements, or moments of emotional distance—can be transformed through patient investment into the relationship's most distinctive and valuable features.

In stark contrast, relationships built on transactional terms resemble speculative trading—marked by unpredictability and instability. Such conditional love, motivated by superficial rewards or immediate pleasure, is akin to high-risk investments that may yield quick profits but often end in losses. Without the steady foundation of devotion, these connections falter when tested by adversity. Their value, tied to fluctuating external factors, diminishes rapidly under pressure, revealing the fragile nature of purely transactional bonds.

Devotional love also operates as a distinct form of currency exchanged between partners—a form not easily devalued by momentary desires or shallow promises. When two individuals trade in this currency, they exchange genuine commitment and sacrifice rather than temporary favors or hollow assurances. This emotional currency, backed by sincerity and integrity, maintains its worth because it is grounded in real intent rather than appearances. The trust cultivated in this exchange becomes a form of wealth that enriches both participants, providing a foundation that resists inflation caused by neglect or betrayal.

A frequent challenge in the realm of love is the confusion between persistence and true commitment. It is all too easy to remain in a relationship simply because much has already been invested—an emotional version of the sunk-cost fallacy. People sometimes cling to partnerships out of a sense of obligation, fear of loss, or the weight of past efforts, rather than from genuine devotion.

But authentic love transcends this trap, recognizing commitment as a conscious choice renewed daily. It is not a burden carried forward by past costs but a deliberate act of nurturing and growth, motivated by hope and belief in the relationship's future.

The daily practice of devotional love can be compared to making regular deposits into an account—small but consistent acts that pay "interest" in the form of deepened trust and intimacy. Listening attentively during difficult conversations, offering forgiveness after misunderstandings, and choosing kindness over resentment all serve to build and maintain the emotional wealth of the partnership. Just as regular contributions sustain financial accounts, these continual efforts are vital for a relationship's health and longevity.

Conversely, neglecting these deposits can create a phenomenon akin to "emotional inflation," where the value of love erodes through withdrawal and indifference. When one or both partners fail to invest time and care, the emotional currency loses its power, leading to cracks in the relationship's foundation. Over time, this neglect can culminate in a collapse similar to an economic downturn, where the accumulated losses overshadow any prior gains. In the marketplace of the heart, confidence and steady investment are essential to prevent such declines.

Just as companies invest in customer relationships knowing that loyal customers provide exponentially more value over time than one-time buyers, devotional love recognizes that consistency builds an irreplaceable bond worth far more than sporadic grand gestures.

Moreover, just like economies, relationships are subject to cycles—periods of growth and contraction influenced by external circumstances and internal dynamics. Career advancements, personal challenges, health issues, and emotional growth all contribute to fluctuations that test the resilience of the bond. In times of downturn, or "recessions," devotional love serves as an anchor, providing stability and reassurance. It is this steadfast devotion that enables partners to navigate uncertainty together, strengthening their alliance in the face of adversity.

Another key aspect of devotional love is the notion of mutual benefit, where the relationship functions as a balanced partnership rather than a zero-sum game. Much like successful economic alliances where both parties contribute resources toward shared goals, this form of love is rooted in trust and cooperation. Partners understand and support each other's needs, aligning their efforts strategically to foster growth and prosperity for both. This mutual investment creates an ecosystem where the well-being of each individual enriches the other, forming a partnership greater than the sum of its parts.

Amazon doesn't just sell products—they own warehouses, delivery trucks, cloud servers, even the cardboard boxes. This vertical integration eliminates middlemen and creates efficiencies competitors can't match. Devotional love pursues similar integration: partners handle conflicts internally rather than outsourcing to friends or family, build private communication channels, and develop exclusive intimacies that create relationship efficiencies no external connection can replicate. This emotional vertical integration reduces transaction costs, eliminates external interference, and creates a self-sustaining ecosystem of mutual support.

Ultimately, devotional love transcends the mere act of giving; it embodies the wisdom of investing in something far more precious than transient pleasure or momentary satisfaction. It transforms relationships from fragile, conditional exchanges into enduring partnerships anchored in shared values and unwavering commitment. This is the true economic model of love—one where both parties thrive not through opportunistic transactions but through dedicated stewardship and faithfulness.

In this chapter, we invite you to reconsider love not just as an emotional experience but as an ongoing investment, a deliberate act of stewardship over the most valuable assets we hold—trust, hope, and connection. To embrace devotional love is to step into the role of both lover and investor, committed over a lifetime to cultivating a bond that stands resilient against the uncertainties of life. It is a secure storehouse for the heart's greatest treasures and a blueprint for enduring companionship through all of life's seasons.

Just as in any economy, where the careful balancing of supply and demand determines stability, devotional love requires an ongoing calibration of giving and receiving between partners. When one partner continually deposits emotional energy and the other withdraws without replenishing, the relationship's balance sheet soon shows signs of distress. Healthy devotional love thrives on reciprocity—not as a rigid ledger of credits and debits but as a dynamic flow, where each partner's generosity feeds the other's growth. This reciprocity builds trust like compound interest: the more you give, the more the relationship yields, encouraging even greater investment.

Like the highways and bridges that enable commerce for generations, the emotional infrastructure built through daily kindnesses creates pathways for deeper connection that serve the relationship for decades to come.

In the world of economics, market confidence is crucial. Investors pour their resources only when they believe in the stability and future potential of their investments. Similarly, devotional love flourishes when both partners have faith—not just in each other but in the relationship itself as a shared enterprise. This confidence is nurtured by consistent actions that demonstrate reliability and care. It is not enough to speak promises; what truly strengthens the bond is the steady demonstration of those promises through everyday acts. Over time, these actions build an emotional credit rating that can weather trials and doubts.

Devotional love also demands strategic patience—a willingness to forgo immediate rewards for longer-term prosperity. In financial markets, investors often resist the temptation to sell at the first sign of volatility, understanding that short-term dips can mask underlying growth. Likewise, those committed to devotional love recognize that challenges and misunderstandings are inevitable parts of any relationship. Rather than reacting impulsively or withdrawing, they maintain their investment of kindness and support, confident that these will pay off in deeper intimacy and resilience.

Wheat farmers use futures contracts to lock in prices months before harvest, protecting against market volatility. Devotional love creates similar futures contracts—promises made today that provide security against tomorrow's uncertainties. These commitments ("in sickness and health," "for better or worse") function like hedging instruments, stabilizing the relationship's value regardless of life's price fluctuations.

Another important economic metaphor here is diversification. Just as wise investors spread their assets across different sectors to mitigate risk, devotional love flourishes when nurtured through various dimensions of connection: emotional, intellectual, physical, and spiritual. Relying solely on one form of affection—such as passion or convenience—can leave the relationship vulnerable to collapse when that element fades. True devotion balances these different forms, ensuring that the relationship remains rich and multifaceted, capable of adapting as circumstances change.

Yet, even the most carefully managed investments require vigilance. Economic downturns come unexpectedly, and so do moments of emotional distance or disconnection. When relationships experience such "market crashes," it is devotional love's steadiness that provides a buffer. Partners who have built a deep reservoir of trust and commitment can weather these storms together, using their shared history and mutual faith as a lifeline. The strength of this foundation makes recovery not only possible but often transformative, allowing the relationship to emerge stronger and more secure than before.

In thinking about love as an economy, it is also crucial to consider the concept of "emotional bankruptcy." Just as businesses can exhaust their resources and become insolvent, relationships can reach a point where neglect and unresolved conflict drain their vitality. Devotional love acts as a safeguard against this by encouraging continuous investment and renewal. It fosters open communication, forgiveness, and the willingness to rebuild trust even after setbacks, preventing the emotional insolvency that can lead to breakdown.

Moreover, the economic metaphor extends to the idea of legacy. Investors often think beyond their own lifetime, considering how their wealth will benefit future generations. Devotional love carries a similar dimension—it builds a relational legacy that transcends the present moment. The values, trust, and emotional wealth cultivated within a partnership ripple outward, influencing families, communities, and even the wider culture. In this sense, devotional love becomes not just a private good but a public asset, contributing to the social fabric with a stability and richness that transactional relationships rarely achieve.

Norway's $1.4 trillion sovereign wealth fund invests oil revenues across global markets, building prosperity for citizens not yet born. The fund's managers think beyond current politicians or economic cycles, focusing on intergenerational wealth. Devotional love adopts this sovereign mindset—building emotional wealth that enriches not just current partners but the families, communities, and legacies they create together. Like Norway's fund managers who balance risk across decades, devoted partners make decisions considering not just immediate happiness but the long-term emotional inheritance they're creating.

This perspective invites us to move beyond a consumerist view of love, where emotions are treated as commodities to be acquired or discarded at will. Instead, it encourages us to see love as a lifelong enterprise requiring active management, strategic foresight, and deep commitment. Just as an experienced investor monitors markets, adjusts portfolios, and seeks counsel, those who embrace devotional love continually reflect on their relationship, nurture its growth, and respond thoughtfully to its needs.

It is also important to recognize that devotional love is not a guarantee of ease or happiness without effort. The most secure investments require ongoing care, vigilance, and sometimes difficult decisions. But the rewards—measured not in fleeting pleasure but in enduring companionship, mutual growth, and shared meaning— are far greater. This kind of love empowers individuals to face life's uncertainties with confidence, knowing they have a partner whose commitment is not dependent on circumstance but rooted in unwavering devotion.

As we continue exploring this theme, it becomes clear that devotional love is as much about stewardship as it is about passion. It calls us to be responsible caretakers of the emotional wealth entrusted to us by our partners and ourselves. It challenges us to invest not only in moments of joy but also in the hard work of reconciliation, patience, and empathy. In doing so, it transforms the economy of the heart into a space of profound abundance, where trust and hope grow exponentially.

The stewardship required in devotional love also involves a deep understanding of risk management. Just as savvy investors assess potential risks and plan contingencies to protect their assets, partners in a devoted relationship must anticipate and navigate emotional challenges with care. Life's uncertainties—stress, misunderstandings, external pressures—can act like market shocks, threatening to destabilize even the strongest bonds. But through clear communication, empathy, and mutual support, couples can build resilience, creating buffers that absorb impact rather than allow fractures.

This proactive approach to relationship care turns devotion into a kind of insurance policy. It's not that problems never arise, but that the emotional capital accumulated through consistent acts of kindness and trust provides a safety net. When conflicts occur, the couple's shared history and commitment enable them to approach issues not as threats but as opportunities for growth and renewal. This perspective shifts the relationship from a fragile venture into a durable partnership where setbacks are not terminal but part of an ongoing cycle of investment and return.

Moreover, understanding devotional love as a complex economy invites us to consider liquidity—the ease with which emotional resources can be accessed and deployed. In financial terms, liquidity ensures that assets can be quickly converted to meet needs without significant loss. Similarly, in a devoted relationship, the ability to express vulnerability, share feelings openly, and seek support functions as emotional liquidity. When partners maintain this fluidity, they can address issues promptly, preventing small problems from crystallizing into enduring barriers.

Toyota's just-in-time manufacturing eliminates waste by delivering components precisely when needed but requires flawless communication between suppliers. Emotional liquidity in devotional love works similarly—partners must fine-tune their ability to provide support exactly when needed, neither overwhelming with premature advice nor withholding when crisis demands immediate response.

Conversely, emotional illiquidity—when partners are unable or unwilling to access and share their inner experiences—can create bottlenecks that disrupt the flow of love. Like frozen assets, these withheld feelings stagnate and reduce the overall health of the relationship's economy. Devotional love, therefore, requires cultivating spaces where openness is encouraged and safe, enabling emotions to circulate freely and nourishing connection.

In proof-of-stake cryptocurrency systems, validators must "stake" their own tokens to participate in network governance—the more they stake, the more influence they have, but also the more they risk losing if they act dishonestly. Devotional love operates on similar principles: partners stake their vulnerability and authenticity to validate the relationship's transactions, earning deeper intimacy but accepting the risk that openness brings.

Another vital aspect is reinvestment. In financial terms, reinvesting earnings allows capital to grow exponentially. In devotional love, reinvestment means using the fruits of past devotion—trust, understanding, shared joy—to fuel further giving. Acts of gratitude, celebration of milestones, and nurturing shared dreams all serve to reinvest emotional wealth back into the relationship. This cyclical process prevents stagnation and promotes a continually flourishing partnership.

This cycle of investment, return, and reinvestment also highlights the transformative power of devotional love. It transcends mere maintenance, becoming a dynamic force that not only preserves the relationship but actively enriches it. Each moment of kindness, patience, and sacrifice compounds to create a legacy of love that shapes the partners' identities and aspirations. They become co-creators of a shared economic ecosystem where abundance is not zero-sum but expansive.

Private equity firms specialize in acquiring struggling companies, then investing intensively in management, operations, and culture to restore profitability. Devotional love employs similar turnaround strategies—when relationships hit distressed periods, partners double down with emotional capital, restructuring communication patterns and rebuilding trust until the partnership emerges stronger and more valuable than before.

It is worth reflecting that many economic models emphasize growth as the ultimate goal, often measured in profit or accumulation. However, devotional love invites us to redefine growth—not as endless acquisition but as deepening connection and shared fulfillment. This growth is qualitative, measured in trust rebuilt after hardship, in the joy of mutual understanding, and in the security that comes from knowing someone is devoted to your well-being through every season of life.

At the same time, this model acknowledges that every economy requires regulation to maintain health and prevent excesses. In relationships, boundaries and ethical commitments serve as these regulations, ensuring that devotion is expressed with respect and honor. Without such guardrails, even the most passionate investments can become reckless, leading to dependency, exploitation, or burnout. True devotional love balances generosity with self-care and mutual respect, creating a sustainable economy of affection.

Sophisticated hedge funds use long/short strategies—betting on some positions while hedging against others—to generate returns regardless of market direction. Devotional love employs similar hedging: celebrating a partner's strengths while gently addressing weaknesses, supporting dreams while managing practical concerns, creating relationship returns that aren't dependent on perfect circumstances.

Finally, this economic metaphor can inspire us to reconsider the way society values different kinds of love. In a culture often obsessed with rapid gratification and transactional interactions, devotional love may seem old-fashioned or impractical. Yet, by framing it as an investment with compounding returns, it gains renewed relevance. It offers a counter-narrative to the volatility of modern relationships, proposing instead a model of stability, growth, and shared prosperity rooted in faith and deliberate care.

Through this lens, devotional love becomes a powerful economic principle that reshapes how we think about connection, commitment, and the use of our emotional resources. It calls us to move beyond superficial exchanges and embrace the challenging but rewarding work of building something lasting and meaningful. By doing so, we contribute not only to our own well-being but to the creation of relational economies that enrich our communities and inspire hope for future generations.

As we reflect on devotional love as a carefully nurtured economic enterprise, it naturally leads us toward a deeper dimension—one where love moves beyond investment and stewardship into the realm of radiant presence. After all, the most profound influence of love is not found merely in transactions or exchanges but in the luminous energy it embodies and transmits. When love is truly devotional, it becomes a force that radiates outward, shaping reality not through argument or persuasion but by simply being.

This transition mirrors the journey from a steady investor to a brand with enduring equity. In business, brand equity is built not just on marketing or sales but on authentic presence—consistent, trustworthy, and resonant. Customers don't need to be convinced to trust a brand that has earned its reputation through genuine value and integrity. Similarly, devotional love, when deeply rooted, creates an influence that cannot be faked or forced. It shines with an authenticity that invites rather than demands, teaching more through presence than through any spoken word.

Radiant love, then, is love as embodied truth. It is living with such alignment between heart, word, and deed that love itself becomes a form of light—illuminating, warming, and inspiring all who come into contact with it. This presence transcends the limitations of conditional exchanges because it emanates from a wellspring within, a reservoir filled by devotion but flowing freely without expectation. It does not seek to convince or control; it simply is, and in that being, it transforms.

To live truthfully is to live in a state where love is visible not as a concept or ideal but as a palpable energy. The influence of such love spreads naturally, like sunlight through leaves or a steady flame in the dark. This love's power lies not in force but in invitation—a silent yet compelling call to authenticity, courage, and connection. Those who embody this love become beacons, not through grand gestures but through the consistent radiance of their presence.

In this way, love's influence is not transactional but transcendental. It is the ultimate form of value a brand holds, both to consumers and the company, earned over time by living with integrity, compassion, and unwavering devotion. The trust it builds is not fragile or fleeting but rooted in the deep knowledge that this love is real and enduring. Others recognize this authenticity instinctively; it cannot be manufactured or imitated. It is the light that reveals what is true and beautiful, often in the smallest moments of genuine care and attention.

Top-tier venture capital deals often involve syndication—where multiple firms join forces, each bringing unique capital and expertise to help a startup thrive. In much the same way, radiant love fosters organically formed networks: extended family, friends, and community members who come together to support a relationship. This shared investment eases the pressure on any one partner and magnifies the couple's collective strength.

Radiant love also introduces a new kind of influence—an economy where power is rooted in vulnerability, and strength is born from openness. It reimagines leadership not as control, but as inspiration—where the impact on others comes from being fully present and authentically oneself. In this light, love becomes a magnetic force, naturally drawing people toward wholeness and hope by simply existing as a living embodiment of those ideals.

Gandhi's transformation of political resistance exemplifies this radiant influence. His concept of satyagraha—"truth-force"—derived its power not from armies or wealth but from his embodied commitment to non-violence and justice. By fasting, spinning cloth, and walking 240 miles to make salt, Gandhi demonstrated that the most profound influence comes from living one's deepest convictions rather than imposing them on others. His presence became a form of moral capital that couldn't be seized or counterfeited—it could only be earned through authentic alignment between belief and action. The British Empire, with all its military might, found itself powerless against someone who wielded influence through vulnerability and whose strength grew from his willingness to suffer for what he loved. Gandhi's example reveals how radiant love operates: it transforms not through force but through the magnetic pull of authenticity, drawing others toward truth by embodying it so completely that resistance becomes irrelevant.

Thus, the bridge from devotional to radiant love is the transformation from committed investment to embodied presence. While devotional love builds the foundation—accumulating trust, nurturing growth, weathering storms—radiant love expresses the flourishing of that foundation as a shining light. It is the natural outcome when love is no longer a transaction or a duty but a lived reality, an influence that moves through the world with grace and power.

In embracing this vision, we are invited to consider not only how we invest our emotional resources but also how we embody the love we have cultivated. The daily acts of kindness, patience, and faithfulness become more than deposits; they become the source of a radiant energy that others can feel and learn from. Our presence becomes a teaching in itself, a living demonstration of what it means to love without condition or calculation.

As you move forward, let this understanding inspire you to cultivate both the economy of devotional love and the luminous presence of radiant love. Together, they form a holistic vision of connection—one grounded in wise stewardship and blossoming into transformative influence. This is love's highest calling: not just to build something lasting but to become a light that guides, uplifts, and changes the world by simply being.

Devotional Love

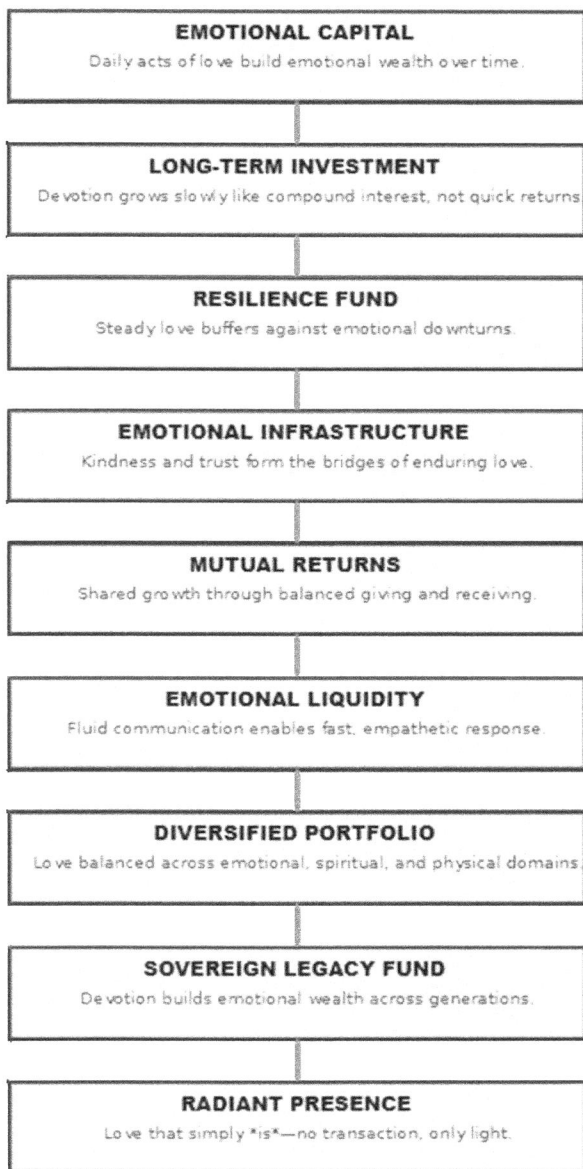

EMOTIONAL CAPITAL

Daily acts of love build emotional wealth over time.

LONG-TERM INVESTMENT

Devotion grows slowly like compound interest, not quick returns.

RESILIENCE FUND

Steady love buffers against emotional downturns.

EMOTIONAL INFRASTRUCTURE

Kindness and trust form the bridges of enduring love.

MUTUAL RETURNS

Shared growth through balanced giving and receiving.

EMOTIONAL LIQUIDITY

Fluid communication enables fast, empathetic response.

DIVERSIFIED PORTFOLIO

Love balanced across emotional, spiritual, and physical domains.

SOVEREIGN LEGACY FUND

Devotion builds emotional wealth across generations.

RADIANT PRESENCE

Love that simply *is*—no transaction, only light.

166

Radiant Love: Embodied Presence and Influence

In the stillness beyond effort, in the soft space where striving dissolves and presence takes root, something subtle and powerful begins to emerge. Love ceases to be a verb, a performance, or a gesture. It becomes essence. Not because it was forced or faked or finely curated, but because it has matured—ripened—into being. This is radiant love: the kind that requires no explanation, no choreography, no permission. It simply shines, because it cannot do otherwise.

Radiant love arises not from impulse, but from integration. It begins, as all true things do, with devotion: that deliberate tending of self and other. In early seasons, love takes the shape of intention—showing up, staying present, choosing compassion even when it's inconvenient. This is the investment phase, when we are still learning how to love, still finding the edges of our ego and softening them into something gentler.

But over time—quietly, almost imperceptibly—the energy shifts. Where once we practiced love, now we become it. The daily disciplines of kindness and care begin to dissolve into us. What felt at first like effort now emerges as ease. The scaffolding disappears, and only the structure remains.

To love radiantly is not to love more or louder or better—it is to love more truly. It is to become a presence in which love is not a decision but a state of being. It is what flows through us when we stop trying to impress, convince, or control. It is the hum beneath the noise. The light in the body. The warmth in the room when nothing has been said but everything is felt.

You can feel the difference. In the presence of someone living in radiant love, there's no push, no pull. No subtle coercion or clever posturing. There's just openness. Spaciousness. A grounded calm that makes it safe to be who you are. It's a kind of energetic integrity—a deep alignment of thought, word, and deed—that transmits something more potent than any sermon or slogan.

That's the thing about radiant love: it doesn't need to speak to be heard. Like sunlight spilling across a windowsill, it makes no argument for its existence. It does not perform its purpose; it is its purpose. It illuminates without judgment, without target, without withholding. It touches everything it reaches—not out of effort, but out of nature.

There's no formula to embody this. You can't fake radiant love. You can't market it or mimic it. What you can do is live in such a way that your presence tells the truth. When you are attuned to what is real—when you are rooted in your body, honest in your speech, and willing to be fully seen—radiance becomes inevitable. Love stops being something you give. It becomes something you are.

That authenticity is what makes radiant love magnetic. We are drawn not to people who are polished or perfect, but to those who are real—who carry themselves with the quiet courage of someone who has nothing to prove. Their influence arises not from their visibility but from their integrity. Not from how loud their voice is, but from how clear their frequency is.

It's important to understand that this kind of influence cannot be hacked or hurried. Brand equity—whether in business or in being—is not accumulated through noise but through resonance. Consistency. Truthfulness. The sense that someone is living their values, not just speaking them. Radiant love earns trust by being itself. And in a world built on appearances, that is nothing short of revolutionary.

While other Roman emperors built monuments to their glory, Marcus Aurelius built something more enduring—a legacy of inner discipline that still influences leaders today. His private journal, the Meditations, wasn't written for publication but as personal reflection during military campaigns. There's no performance in these pages, no imperial posturing—just a powerful man wrestling honestly with power, mortality, and duty. His soldiers followed him not because he demanded loyalty through fear, but because they witnessed a leader who held himself to higher standards than he asked of others. When plague ravaged the empire and barbarian tribes pressed the borders, Marcus didn't retreat to luxury—he stayed with his troops, demonstrating the very stoicism he practiced in private. His influence transcended his reign because it wasn't built on spectacle but on the quiet consistency of a man aligned with his principles.

So much of modern life is built around performance. Influence is chased through algorithms, attention begged for in the currency of likes and metrics. But radiant love doesn't chase. It doesn't hustle for approval. It does not twist itself into strategies or scale its soul to fit the feed. It simply is. And in being itself, it draws others back to themselves.

This isn't passive. It's power. It's what happens when love is no longer filtered through fear. When you stop shaping your identity to avoid rejection and start living from the inside out. That shift—from fear-based performance to truth-based presence—is what makes radiant love possible. It's the difference between impressing someone and impacting them. Between saying the right thing and being the real thing.

When Václav Havel walked into Prague's smoky theaters in the 1970s, he wasn't strategizing revolution—he was simply writing truth. As communist authorities banned his plays and imprisoned him repeatedly, something remarkable happened: his quiet persistence became more powerful than any propaganda. Havel never raised his voice or called for uprising. Instead, he wrote essays like "The Power of the Powerless" from his authentic experience of living under oppression. His words carried the weight of lived truth rather than political rhetoric. When the Berlin Wall fell, citizens didn't rally around a charismatic demagogue—they gravitated toward this soft-spoken playwright who had spent decades embodying the very freedom he wrote about. Havel's influence wasn't manufactured; it emerged from years of choosing truth over safety, integrity over comfort. He toppled an empire not through force but through the magnetic pull of authenticity.

Think of those rare people who seem to carry a kind of stillness with them, a presence that slows the room, softens the air. You can't always name what it is, but you feel it. There's no ego in it, no spotlight. Just an unshakable calm that seems to say: "You're safe here." That is radiant love at work—not as sentiment, but as embodiment. Not as something projected outward, but as something arising from deep within.

Reflect on Maria Montessori entering her first classroom in Rome's San Lorenzo slums. While educators imposed rigid discipline on "unteachable" children, Montessori simply removed obstacles and created space. She didn't command attention—she quietly worked with materials at a small table. Without instruction, restless children gravitated toward her presence. She wasn't performing education; she had become it. Her centered attention created a field where natural curiosity could emerge. Children labeled as problems revealed themselves as eager learners, not because she fixed them but because her unconditional regard allowed their true nature to surface. Teachers worldwide came not to copy techniques but to experience what authentic presence felt like. They left transformed, carrying that same quality to their own classrooms—ripples of influence born not from strategy but from being fully aligned with purpose.

This is the love that teaches without teaching. The presence that invites without pushing. The energy that holds space for transformation simply by existing fully. And its impact—though often subtle—is immeasurable. Like light filtering through leaves, it changes everything it touches, even if it leaves no trace you can point to.

To reach this state isn't about mastering others. It's about mastering your alignment. Radiant love comes from being at peace with yourself—not a performance of peace, but the real thing. A peace rooted in acceptance, forged through honesty, and upheld by devotion. The kind of peace that doesn't break when the world disappoints you. The kind that endures because it isn't built on anything external.

Living in radiant love means relinquishing the need to control how you're perceived. It means choosing to live truthfully, not performatively. It's about trusting that your presence—your actual, unfiltered, vulnerable presence—is enough. More than enough. It's the medicine the world didn't know it needed until you offered it simply by being real.

The transformation from effortful love to radiant being is not a straight line. It bends, stalls, loops back. There are days when presence feels natural and others when it seems unreachable. But even in those faltering steps, the seed of radiance continues to grow. Because this form of love is not destroyed by struggle; in fact, it often deepens in the face of it. Every time we choose honesty over pretense, stillness over reactivity, acceptance over control—we feed the flame within.

To live in radiant love is to let go of performance. We shed the need to be impressive, to be admired, to be right. These are the echoes of an insecure self trying to confirm its worth through others' eyes. But radiant love begins when we realize we are already enough—not because we've achieved something or won approval but because we exist, truthfully and fully. There is a profound liberation in that knowing. Once you understand it, your entire way of being begins to shift. You stop looking outward for validation. You begin to trust your own inner compass. And gradually, the fear that used to cloud your interactions begins to lift.

It is not always comfortable. In fact, this kind of inner shift often brings a period of discomfort. It strips away the masks we once wore for protection. And without them, we feel exposed—sometimes painfully so. But it is in this very rawness that light enters. The light of truth. The light of who we are without distortion. And once that light takes hold, even our pain becomes part of the radiance. It becomes transmuted—not erased, but integrated, softened by the grace of presence.

When you begin living from that place, the way you move through the world changes. Your conversations carry a different tone. You are less reactive, more curious. You listen not to respond but to truly hear. You no longer need to dominate a room to be felt within it. You simply arrive—and your presence does the rest.

People may not always understand it. Some may find your groundedness unsettling. Others might misread your calm as aloofness, or your refusal to engage in drama as disinterest. But that is not your concern, because radiant love is not a strategy. It is not aimed at pleasing or persuading. It simply exists—as you do—unapologetically and with quiet certainty.

And there will be those who see you, really see you. Not because you performed your worth, but because your authenticity gave them permission to see their own. These connections are rare, but they are luminous. They do not cling or control; they inspire and liberate. And they remind you that, even in a fragmented world, truth recognizes truth.

In this way, radiant love is not just something you give—it becomes something you are. And being in that state is itself a form of giving. Every moment lived in authenticity becomes an offering. Every silent act of integrity becomes a gift. Not because it's noticed or rewarded, but because it's real.

When Jane Addams opened Hull House in Chicago's immigrant slums in 1889, she didn't arrive with grand proclamations about social reform. Instead, she simply moved into the neighborhood and began living among the people she hoped to serve. While other reformers lectured from platforms about the poor, Addams learned their languages, ate their food, and listened to their stories. She didn't impose solutions—she created space where immigrants could preserve their dignity while adapting to American life. Hull House became a sanctuary not because Addams preached about justice, but because justice flowed through her daily actions. She offered childcare not as charity but as recognition of working mothers' needs. She provided English classes not to erase culture but to open doors. Her influence grew organically as lives were transformed, one conversation, one family, one generation at a time. Politicians and philanthropists eventually sought her counsel not because she campaigned for attention, but because her results spoke louder than any rhetoric.

The influence you carry in this state is different from what the world often teaches. It doesn't come from credentials, titles, or volume. It flows from coherence—the alignment between your inner world and your outer actions. People feel it more than they see it. They are drawn not to your ideas alone but to the energy those ideas arise from. They sense the depth beneath your words, the stillness behind your presence.

Rachel Carson spent her mornings walking the shores of Maine, notebook in hand, observing the intricate relationships between species most people never noticed. When she began writing Silent Spring, she wasn't mounting a crusade—she was simply documenting what she saw: birds falling silent, fish dying, ecosystems collapsing under the weight of pesticides. Carson didn't shout or sensationalize; she wrote with the careful precision of a scientist and the lyrical beauty of a poet who truly loved the natural world. Her book didn't attack industries or individuals—it revealed consequences with such clarity that readers couldn't unsee what she showed them. Chemical companies fought back with personal attacks and scientific challenges, but Carson's influence endured because it was rooted in observable truth rather than ideology. She sparked the modern environmental movement not through activism but through the magnetic power of someone who had spent decades in authentic relationship with the living world, translating that intimacy into words that made others care.

This effect does not bend others to your will—it invites them into their own. It awakens a memory, long buried perhaps, of what it feels like to live sincerely. And that invitation, unspoken but deeply felt, has the power to transform more than arguments or advice ever could.

Radiant love doesn't require perfection. In fact, it thrives in our imperfections—so long as we are honest about them. Vulnerability, when grounded in truth, is not weakness; it is strength without armor. When we admit what we don't know, own our missteps, and show our scars without shame, we become accessible. We become human in the truest, most beautiful sense.

To live in that space is to stop trying to be extraordinary and instead to be profoundly ordinary—with extraordinary presence. And it is often in the most mundane of moments—a quiet walk, a shared glance, a kind word—that radiance reveals itself most clearly.

It doesn't demand ceremony. It doesn't need an audience. It only asks that you show up—fully, consistently, and with an open heart. And over time, these small acts of presence add up. They form a legacy—not the kind etched in stone or shouted from rooftops, but the kind felt in the quiet transformation of lives touched by yours.

That is what radiant love offers: not power over others but power within. A power that neither inflates the ego nor hides behind humility, but simply is. A power that grows not from control, but from surrender—surrender to truth, to presence, to the gentle unfolding of your most authentic self.

This unfolding is not always dramatic. Sometimes, it feels like nothing is happening at all. But something always is. Every choice to stay grounded, every breath taken with intention, every moment where you choose love over fear—it all builds the field of light around you. And over time, you become that light. Not in a symbolic sense, but in a real, felt way.

It becomes easier to forgive, because you are less attached to being right. It becomes easier to be generous, because you are no longer measuring what is owed. It becomes easier to be still, because you no longer fear what silence might reveal. And this ease is not laziness—it is grace. It is what emerges when effort is replaced by alignment.

In the same way a brand accumulates equity through trust and consistency, so too does a person. Radiant love builds its own kind of brand equity—not in markets or metrics, but in hearts and memories. It is not manufactured; it is accrued. Each moment of integrity, each honest act, each time we remain present in discomfort, we invest in that equity. We show others, and ourselves, that our energy is reliable—that we are what we appear to be.

Authentic energy cannot be faked. It cannot be rushed. It is not charisma or charm. It is not the gloss of inspiration or the spike of motivation. It is the steady current of truth running beneath the surface, visible in the smallest things: how we listen, how we pause, how we treat someone who can offer us nothing. And over time, that current is felt by those around us—not as a campaign or a pitch, but as presence. And presence builds influence—the real kind, the enduring kind. Not influence that manipulates, but influence that resonates.

In this way, radiant love becomes the foundation of personal credibility. Not because it makes us agreeable or universally liked, but because it makes us clear. People may not always agree with you, but they will know where you stand. They will trust your essence, even if they question your ideas. And that trust is gold in a world saturated with noise.

We earn that trust not by branding ourselves with clever words, but by becoming the energy we claim to represent. The more aligned we are internally, the less we need to convince externally. The more we embody truth, the more influence flows—naturally, effortlessly.

Think of radiant love as spiritual brand equity. It accumulates slowly. It compounds through consistency. It grows strongest not during our highs but in how we navigate our lows. It is not measured in followers or applause, but in how deeply others feel seen in our presence. Because when your love radiates without an agenda, it becomes a mirror. Others glimpse themselves more clearly in it— and that reflection, that rare, unfiltered glimpse, is a gift few forget.

You don't have to shout to be heard when your energy speaks for you. You don't have to persuade when your being already transmits a signal of truth. And in a world where most signals are distorted, that signal becomes magnetic.

But this is not about personal branding in the superficial sense. Radiant love is not an image we polish; it's a frequency we embody. It's not about controlling how we are perceived, but releasing control altogether. Because the most powerful energy is not curated—it is lived. Moment by moment, word by word, breath by breath.

And yes, this kind of influence can change rooms. It can shift dynamics. It can create space for honesty in conversations that would otherwise remain guarded. But perhaps more importantly, it changes us. It teaches us that we do not need to perform in order to matter. That we do not need to strategize in order to lead. That love—steady, unforced, and radiant—is strategy enough.

That's the paradox. The more we release the desire to be influential, the more influence we carry. Because people remember energy more than arguments. They remember how we made them feel far more than what we said. And when our energy leaves them feeling grounded, empowered, or safe, they trust us—even if they cannot articulate why.

This is the true return on the investment of authentic love. It creates a ripple that moves quietly but thoroughly through the fabric of connection. It doesn't demand loyalty—it earns it. It doesn't manufacture followers—it awakens leaders. And in this way, the quiet power of radiant love begins to reshape the culture around it— not through domination, but through resonance.

You become less interested in impressing and more focused on aligning. Less drawn to competition and more drawn to coherence. You realize that energy does the heavy lifting when words fall short. That silence, when full of presence, speaks volumes. And that authenticity, when practiced consistently, builds a reputation more durable than any performance could.

So, the work becomes this: to keep returning to truth, even when it costs us. To keep radiating love, even when it is misunderstood. To keep showing up—especially when it's easier to withdraw. And in doing so, we build equity—not for gain, but for good. Not for recognition, but for resonance.

And when the time comes that someone reaches for your presence, not because of what you offer, but because of who you are, you'll know: the equity has accumulated. Not in numbers, but in depth. Not in visibility, but in value.

And there is no metric more meaningful than that.

When radiant love becomes a lived truth, it does not stay contained. Its nature is not static. It multiplies—not through force or strategy, but by its very architecture. The more authentically love is lived, the more it invites reflection. It moves through systems not as noise but as signal. And here, we begin to touch the next dimension of love: its fractal nature.

Fractal love is the recognition that love scales. That the smallest, most personal act of care is not isolated—it belongs to a pattern. Just as a single spiral in nature reflects the same geometry found in galaxies, a single moment of loving presence reflects and reinforces a universal structure. What begins as an internal resonance moves outward in waves, echoing through networks seen and unseen.

Every loving interaction, however brief, imprints something. It leaves a mark—not just on the person receiving it, but on the field of possibility itself. That one act becomes a new seed, capable of taking root elsewhere. A kind word, an act of grace, an unseen forgiveness—these are not minor. They are signatures of the pattern, carriers of the code.

In distributed systems, small actions taken by independent nodes can result in global coherence. The same is true in love. When lived authentically and without demand, love teaches by its very presence. It inspires without effort. And more than that—it replicates. It embeds a new pattern into the environment, one that others can sense, learn, and echo in their own way.

You might never witness the full reach of your love. You might not see how one moment of tenderness becomes the reason someone else chose kindness over harm, how one steady presence gave another the courage to show up differently the next day. But this is not a loss—it is the nature of fractal love: it does not require recognition to scale.

Just as the structure of a tree repeats in its branches, its leaves, its roots, the structure of love repeats across the landscapes of connection. Each loving moment reflects the larger shape of the whole. This is why love is never wasted. Even in solitude. Even in silence. Even when the world doesn't seem to notice.

The repetition of love across scales is not linear—it is exponential. One aligned moment multiplies. One individual living truthfully influences many, who then influence others. You don't have to build a movement; you are already part of one. The movement of energy, of intention, of presence. It is distributed across time and people, like a network that hums with resonance once enough nodes begin to sing the same tone.

Mother Teresa never strategized about global influence while washing the wounds of dying strangers in Calcutta's slums. She simply showed up, day after day, treating each forgotten person as sacred. Her sisters watched this radical presence and began replicating it—not the actions, but the quality of attention. Volunteers came not for the cause but to witness what unconditional love looked like in practice. They left transformed, carrying that same reverence back to their own corners of the world. Her work scaled not through expansion but through inspiration: one authentic heart teaching others what was possible when love became embodied rather than proclaimed.

The idea of influence as brand equity—earned through consistent authenticity—finds its echo here too. In fractal love, your presence is your message. Your life becomes your signal. It spreads not through amplification but through coherence. When enough people align with that energy, change happens—not as spectacle, but as shift. Quiet. Powerful. Irreversible.

By the 1990s, Johnny Cash's career seemed finished—a relic dismissed by country radio and ignored by younger audiences. Then producer Rick Rubin stripped away the polish and let Cash's weathered voice tell raw truth. The "American Recordings" series wasn't a manufactured comeback—it was authentic essence finally finding its proper form. Cash's covers of contemporary songs became profound because they carried the weight of a life fully lived. His influence grew not through reinvention but through deeper alignment with who he'd always been. A new generation discovered him not as nostalgia but as timeless authenticity, proving that truth resonates across all boundaries when it's genuinely embodied.

And so, radiant love becomes a gateway, a doorway into the deeper reality that love is not just emotion, not just connection, but a self-replicating principle. It scales across individuals, communities, generations. The pattern repeats. The light continues. And even after we are gone, the shape of our love remains—written into the lives we touched, the spaces we softened, the energy we carried.

This is legacy. Not legacy in the historical sense, but in the living sense, in the now. You are never too small to impact the whole. A single sincere act, done without audience, can be the spark that lights a vast field. Love is not limited by size. It is not constrained by circumstance. Its pattern is infinite. And every time we align with it, we contribute to its unfolding.

In this way, love asks for both presence and perspective: to live it fully here, now, and to know that here and now belong to a larger shape. That our truth echoes into others. That our integrity becomes part of a long, unbroken thread stretching across stories and lifetimes.

Radiant love becomes fractal love when we realize this: that being true in one moment is being true for all moments, that each act carries the signature of all others, that we are not isolated nodes trying to make a difference—but interconnected expressions of the same source, repeating the same beauty in countless forms.

So, we begin where we are. We speak truthfully. We act kindly. We stay rooted in what is real. And through us, love scales—not by volume, but by vibration. Not by controlling outcomes, but by transmitting essence.

And in doing so, we don't just love—we become love. Not as feeling, not as identity, but as structure. As pattern. As presence that teaches without speaking, heals without claiming, and multiplies without end.

Because the true mark of radiant love is not how brightly it burns in the moment—but how quietly it continues in the lives it touches.

Radiant Love

DEVOTION
Deliberate tending of self and other.
Love takes the shape of intention.

INTEGRATION
Daily disciplines dissolve into being.
Where effort transforms into ease through practice.

AUTHENTICITY
Living truthfully, not performatively.
Releasing the need to control how you're perceived.

PRESENCE
Grounded calm making it safe to be who you are.
Energetic integrity—alignment of thought.

RESONANCE
Influence arises from frequency.
Brand equity built through true consistency.

REFLECTION
Authentic love becomes a mirror for others.
Inviting others into their own truth by your example.

FRACTALIZATION
Love scales through pattern replication.
Moments multiplies across networks of connection.

Fractal Love: Patterns Reflecting the Whole

In the vast, sprawling landscape of human experience, love often appears elusive—a flicker on the edge of perception, an ideal we chase but seldom grasp in full. And yet, what if the secret to love isn't hidden in mystery at all, but in the very patterns that shape our world? What if love is not just a feeling but a structure—one that replicates, scales, and sustains like a fractal? A pattern that, when seen clearly, reveals that the smallest, simplest acts of care are not only meaningful in their own right, but also microcosms of something much larger.

This way of understanding love—as a fractal—shifts everything. In mathematics and in nature, fractals are patterns that repeat at every scale. Whether you zoom in on the branching of a tree or pull back to view the sweep of a river delta, the same recursive forms emerge. There's elegance in this repetition, and more importantly, there's truth. When we begin to see love this way—as a pattern that shows up across layers—we uncover its quiet power: the power of small, consistent gestures to ripple outward, shaping not just lives but entire systems, entire epochs.

At first glance, love seems too grand, too elusive to be reduced to such structures. But if you look more closely, you begin to see how love inhabits form. A smile held longer than necessary, a word spoken with care, a moment of patience in the midst of frustration—these are not trivial. They are fragments of a greater whole, iterations of a deeper rhythm. When someone chooses to forgive, to comfort, to simply listen without judgment, they're not performing isolated acts. They're contributing to a broader geometry of trust and connection. The same way a single leaf reflects the shape of its tree, each of these moments reflects love in its entirety.

This is not just poetry—it's systems thinking. If we view love as a distributed network, a living system of intention and attention, each interaction becomes a node in a vast web. In this network, no act is insignificant because each act carries the potential to propagate. In computing, distributed systems rely on principles of redundancy, replication, and scalability. They are built to resist failure, to persist, and to adapt. Love, seen as a living distributed system, mirrors this resilience. Each act of kindness is a replication. Each gesture of compassion reinforces a connection, building networks strong enough to hold communities together, especially in times of fracture.

Think of how successful companies build customer loyalty through consistent micro-interactions: a thoughtful follow-up email, remembering a client's preference, addressing concerns promptly—these small touchpoints create trust networks that scale exponentially. Like fractals, each positive interaction contains the DNA of the entire customer relationship, building enterprise value through accumulated care.

We often speak of love in grandiose terms—romance, sacrifice, redemption—but in truth, love flourishes in the micro. The beauty of a fractal is not in the spectacle of its outer edges, but in the intricacy of its repetition. So it is with love. A parent's lullaby sung each night forms a rhythm that echoes through generations. A neighbor's decision to check in on an elderly friend becomes part of a local ecosystem of care. These acts are fractal. They scale. And when enough of them are patterned together, they become culture.

There is something profoundly humbling in this realization. It means that love is never out of reach, never reserved for the extraordinary. It is ordinary by design—and it's this very ordinariness that makes it so powerful. Love doesn't wait for permission to act; it simply acts. It shows up in text messages sent at the right time, in meals cooked without expectation, in the ways we stand beside one another during illness or uncertainty. Each of these is a fractal form, each reflecting the whole.

Even in times of distance and digital mediation, this pattern persists. Think of how messages of support travel through online networks during moments of collective grief or global crisis: one post, one share, one word of encouragement. They replicate, they reinforce, they form invisible bridges across time zones and cultural boundaries. The pattern scales—faster than ever—and reminds us that no node in the network is alone.

But love isn't just scalable in reach; it's scalable in depth. It contains recursive layers of meaning. The way a child experiences love in the home sets the tone for how they relate to the world. That foundation then gets mirrored in how they offer care to friends, partners, and communities. Small dynamics carry forward, shaped by context but powered by repetition. A kind word today may become a guiding principle tomorrow. The child becomes the parent. The comforted becomes the comforter. The pattern repeats—not identically, but recognizably.

Economic systems mimic this recursive pattern. A mentor's investment in one entrepreneur creates ripple effects—that entrepreneur mentors others, who build companies, create jobs, and foster innovation. Each mentorship decision functions like compound interest, where small initial investments of guidance and support generate exponential returns across entire economic ecosystems over decades.

And because love replicates, it endures—not as something frozen in time, but as a rhythm that flows across generations. The tenderness of an ancestor may live on in your habits, your choices, your voice. What someone once gave freely—perhaps with little acknowledgment—may still be shaping the emotional architecture of your life. That is the quiet, miraculous power of fractal love: it doesn't need to be seen to be real. It just needs to be repeated.

This perspective also demands something of us. It asks us to be more than passive recipients of love—it invites us to become mindful participants in its pattern. Once we see how it scales, we also see how responsible we are for continuing the rhythm. Every decision becomes a chance to either reinforce or interrupt the pattern. We can choose to replicate love or replicate indifference. The pattern doesn't enforce itself; it is made, day by day, act by act.

To live fractally—to love fractally—is to live with awareness of this repetition. It is to cultivate what might be called "fractal mindfulness," a commitment to understanding how even the smallest gestures reflect and influence systems beyond our view. It is to recognize the sacred geometry of daily kindness. And it is to trust that the ripple you begin here and now may one day shape a future you'll never see.

We don't need to engineer grand legacies. We need only to participate fully and lovingly in the moment in front of us, and to trust in the replication.

Love, when understood as a fractal, reveals a profound hidden order beneath our often chaotic and unpredictable experiences. It shows us that patterns of care, generosity, and connection aren't isolated flukes or momentary sparks—they are echoes of a much deeper rhythm running through everything. Just as a fern's leaf mimics the form of the entire plant, the smallest expression of love contains within it the possibility of immense significance.

There is something quietly revolutionary about realizing that love is not dependent on scale to have impact. The hug offered to a grieving friend, the food prepared with care, the text sent just to check in—each act contains within it the whole architecture of what love means. These moments don't diminish in value because they're small. Quite the opposite: their intimacy allows them to be carried deeply within us, altering the architecture of our inner selves, shaping how we relate to others, and gradually tilting the balance of entire systems.

To view love through a fractal lens is to begin noticing that no act is too small to matter. It is to feel the gravity of presence when listening without distraction. It is to value sincerity over performance, not because the scale is less but because the intention reverberates. And intention, like the initial input in a recursive equation, determines the trajectory of the pattern that follows.

The implications of this shift in perspective are immense. In a society trained to valorize big gestures, flashy headlines, and grand declarations, we often overlook the quieter revolutions happening through the micro gestures of everyday love. A child learning they are safe. A stranger being met with dignity. A couple navigating conflict with softness. These are not stories told in newspapers, but they are the foundation upon which all broader social transformation rests. Every movement that ever changed the world began with an individual deciding to act lovingly, even when it was inconvenient.

Systems thinking gives us language for this. In complex networks, a small change in one part can produce a disproportionately large impact elsewhere. This phenomenon, known as emergence, is evident in ecosystems, economies—and human relationships. A kind act can shift the tone of a day, the culture of a group, even the trajectory of a family. When love is practiced recursively—when we model the love we've received and reflect it outward—it spreads organically through this networked system we call society.

Carpet manufacturer Ray Anderson's sustainability awakening began with reading Paul Hawken's The Ecology of Commerce. This single moment of consciousness led to Mission Zero—eliminating environmental footprint by 2020. The decision rippled through every supplier, competitor, and industry standard. Interface's fractal approach to regenerative business influenced thousands of companies to adopt circular economy principles, transforming entire manufacturing sectors.

The analogy of distributed systems is particularly helpful here. In computing, distributed systems operate not through centralized control, but through nodes that work together—each contributing to the overall resilience, functionality, and adaptability of the system. When one node strengthens its ability to send and receive meaningful data, the whole network benefits. In the same way, when one person becomes more attuned to the practice of love, it improves the emotional bandwidth of their entire environment. They become a node of trust, reliability, and care—and others, in turn, are influenced.

Brazilian CEO Ricardo Semler dismantled traditional hierarchy, allowing employees to set their own salaries and work schedules. This radical trust experiment created a fractal of autonomy—each empowered employee became a decision-making node, strengthening the entire network. Semco's revenue grew 900%, while competitors struggled, proving that distributed love-based leadership creates exponentially stronger organizational resilience than command and control structures.

LinkedIn's professional networking exemplifies this fractal principle. One meaningful connection leads to introductions, collaborations, and opportunities that ripple outward. A single thoughtful recommendation or shared insight can influence career trajectories across multiple degrees of separation, demonstrating how individual acts of professional generosity scale into thriving business ecosystems.

This idea also invites us to look at generational love in a new way. Think of how trauma is often said to be passed down—patterns of fear, reactivity, neglect. But the same mechanism works for healing and love. When someone interrupts a cycle of harm—choosing gentleness where they once experienced violence, offering understanding where there was once indifference—they plant new seeds. These seeds don't only grow in one relationship; they create new possibilities for all those connected to them. And the beauty of fractals is that change at any level reshapes the whole.

In families, we often see this most clearly. The way a parent speaks to their child in a moment of frustration might echo the way they themselves were spoken to decades earlier. But when that cycle is interrupted with mindfulness—with a conscious choice toward love—it shifts the entire structure. That child may grow up with a fundamentally different internal landscape, which then informs their friendships, their parenting, their leadership. It is in this way that love becomes transgenerational, not only in story but in cellular memory.

When Merck developed a cure for river blindness but African patients couldn't afford it, CEO Roy Vagelos made an unprecedented decision: give the drug away free forever. This act of corporate compassion created a fractal of pharmaceutical generosity—inspiring industry wide access programs, influencing WHO policies, and establishing new models of global health equity that continue healing millions across generations.

And we need not only look backward. Love's recursive potential also invites us to be future oriented. To ask: What kind of echoes do I want my actions to leave behind? What am I seeding in this moment that might one day grow into a forest of connection I may never see? This mindset humbles us and empowers us at once. It reminds us that we are never acting in isolation, even when it feels that way.

When Gravitas Ventures began sharing complete financial statements with filmmakers—showing exact revenues, expenses, and profit margins—it shattered Hollywood's culture of financial opacity. In an industry where distributors traditionally kept creators in the dark about their own film's performance, this radical transparency seemed like competitive suicide. Instead, it created a fractal of trust that transformed the entire filmmaker relationship. Directors and producers began choosing Gravitas specifically for this honesty, leading to higher quality submissions and stronger partnerships. The transparency model expanded outward, pressuring competitors to adopt similar practices and inspiring new platforms built on open book principles, proving that vulnerable honesty can become a competitive advantage.

There is a quiet responsibility in this awareness. When you understand that your loving presence today might shape someone else's capacity to offer love tomorrow, you begin to move differently. It becomes less about being perfect and more about being intentional. Less about control, more about contribution. You begin to recognize yourself as a participant in a much larger choreography—one that spans time, geography, and identity.

Fractals also teach us about resilience. The beauty of self similarity is that even when part of a pattern is damaged, the whole can regenerate. Similarly, love has the capacity to repair what has been broken—not by erasing pain, but by integrating it into something more whole. When we bring love into painful spaces, we do not undo the past, but we shape how it's carried. We reframe the narrative. We introduce the possibility of renewal.

This is why even a single act can matter. Why even a flicker of kindness in a moment of despair can become the hinge on which a life turns. We often imagine transformation as dramatic, but more often, it is quiet. Gradual. Fractal.

And this understanding removes the pressure to be extraordinary. To participate in the pattern of love, you need not do something grand. You need only be willing to reflect what has been reflected to you—to become one more link in the chain, one more heartbeat in the rhythm.

So love, as a fractal, is not something we aspire to reach in some distant future. It is a pattern we are already part of. Every time we speak gently, offer presence, extend generosity—we mirror the whole. And the more we recognize this mirroring, the more deliberate we become in the pattern we reflect.

In seeing love as fractal, we begin to understand that love is not only something we give, or feel, or receive—it is something we become. Through conscious repetition of small acts, through pattern making across time, love begins to rewire us. Not just in the poetic sense, but quite literally—our neural pathways adjust, our instincts recalibrate. What once felt difficult—vulnerability, patience, presence—can become our new default. And this is not the result of one grand transformation, but of many, many small ones, layered like rings in a tree, marking every season of growth.

There is a grace in understanding this: you don't need to have it all figured out to be part of the pattern. You just need to be willing to start. And start again. And again. Love, when viewed fractally, is forgiving in its architecture—it allows us to return, to rebuild, to revise. It expects iteration, not perfection.

Consider the practice of repair. In most relationships, even the loving ones, there are ruptures—misunderstandings, betrayals, silences, sharp words. We often think of these as setbacks, but in a fractal model, they are part of the structure itself. Repair is not a deviation from love—it is love.

When seven people died from cyanide laced Tylenol, J&J immediately recalled 31 million bottles nationwide—losing $100 million instantly. This radical act of putting customer safety over profits became the gold standard for crisis management. The pattern of choosing care over cost rippled through decades of corporate decisions, building unshakeable consumer trust that now generates billions in brand value.

The willingness to mend, to return to each other, to say "I was wrong" or "I see you now" or "Let's try again"—these are recursive acts that deepen the pattern. They make it richer, more resilient. Just as a coastline gains its jagged beauty from the way the waves have worn it over time, relationships gain depth from how they have weathered.

CVS Health abandoned $2 billion in annual tobacco revenue to align with their healthcare mission. This radical act of corporate integrity—choosing values over profits—flowed through the entire healthcare retail sector. Competitors followed suit, insurance companies offered incentives, and public health improved measurably. The fractal effect of one company's moral courage reshaped an entire industry's relationship with health.

Market leaders understand this principle of resilient iteration. Companies like Toyota built their reputation through continuous improvement (kaizen)—each small refinement in process or product quality compounds over time. Failed experiments aren't setbacks but data points that strengthen the overall system, much like how relationship repairs deepen trust through demonstrated commitment to growth.

When we lean into this way of thinking, we stop fearing the cracks. We begin to understand that love is not the absence of struggle, but the willingness to stay through it, to choose again, to reflect, adjust, and keep going. And in this way, love evolves—not in a linear path, but in spirals, each cycle bringing us closer to something both new and familiar.

This spiral nature is deeply tied to healing. Healing, too, is not a destination but a pattern. We revisit old wounds not because we are stuck, but because each time we come back to them, we bring new insight, new capacity, new compassion. We spiral back with more perspective. The hurt may still be there, but we carry it differently; we surround it with more understanding. And this, too, is an act of love—toward ourselves and others.

It is important to say here that not all love is soft. Sometimes, love is boundary. Sometimes, love is walking away. Sometimes, it is silence or space, or refusal. To imagine love as a fractal does not mean it is always warm and welcoming—it means it is always intentional, that it mirrors the conditions for growth, even when that growth requires difficulty. A parent might set a limit out of love. A friend might speak a hard truth. A partner might end a relationship to preserve what dignity remains. These are not breaks from love—they are acts of clarity within it.

In a fractal framework, even endings carry echoes. Even absences leave shape. What matters is the pattern we choose to repeat after those endings. Do we carry the pain forward as punishment, or do we integrate it into a wiser, wider self? Do we continue the cycle of harm, or do we become a new node—a place where the pattern changes?

To take responsibility for our own pattern is to begin crafting the world we want to live in. It is to stop waiting for others to be more kind, more fair, more loving—and instead to embody those things ourselves, first and repeatedly. Not to be martyrs or saints, but to be citizens of a relational world. Because every system we belong to—family, friendship, community, society—is made of these micro choices: people deciding, again and again, whether to protect or exploit, to soften or harden, to show up or retreat.

This is the true work of love: not grand gestures, but the steady, quiet calibration. The showing up with care. The choosing to communicate even when it's awkward. The listening even when we're tired. The being accountable even when we're ashamed. Love is not a mood or a moment—it's a practice. A recursive one. And like any practice, it builds over time.

Fractal love also challenges us to widen our lens, to understand that the same pattern playing out in our personal relationships exists on a social level, too. How we relate to our neighbors, how we talk to strangers, how we treat service workers or the unhoused or the elderly—these are not separate from love. They are love, scaled outward. The fractal grows.

When enough people live this way—consciously, relationally, lovingly—a culture begins to shift. Not overnight, not dramatically, but steadily. Institutions become less cruel. Norms become more compassionate. Policies reflect care. And while no single act is sufficient, every act is significant. Because in a fractal, every piece contains the whole.

So what does this mean for us, practically? It means we stop waiting for a feeling to arrive and start making a choice. It means we reflect on our patterns—of speech, of listening, of conflict, of silence—and ask: What am I repeating? What am I building? What am I teaching through my presence? It means we resist the urge to categorize people as good or bad, worthy or not—and instead ask what love looks like in this moment, with this person, in this context.

And then we act—imperfectly, yes, sometimes clumsily, but with intention.

We don't do this alone. The fractal nature of love means that every shift we make is mirrored somewhere else. Every time you choose empathy over ego, someone near you feels safer. Every time you apologize sincerely, someone learns that they can, too. Every time you tell the truth kindly, you create a crack in the armor of shame that so many wear.

In this way, we become each other's pattern. We become the evidence that love is possible—on hard days, in broken systems, across differences. We are the texture of love. The living proof.

And maybe, just maybe, that's enough.

If we are each other's pattern, then we are also each other's reflections. We echo back not just presence but possibility. When someone shows us kindness when we expected indifference—or grace when we expected judgment—it disrupts the loop. It introduces a new variable, and if we are open, it reshapes the equation. Love becomes contagious, not in a sentimental way, but in the deeply mathematical sense: small changes, repeated across systems, yield exponential results.

This is not always visible. In fact, it's usually not. The most meaningful acts of love often go unacknowledged: the message sent when you knew someone was lonely, the tone you softened even though you were hurting, the effort to understand instead of escalate. No applause. No spotlight. But in a fractal world, those acts ripple. They influence the pattern in ways we may never see. Just because we cannot trace the line does not mean it was never drawn.

This is why cynicism, though seductive, is incomplete. It may be honest about the world's harms, but it fails to account for the complexity of repair. Love, when practiced fractally, is not naïve— it is strategic. It builds systems of care within systems of harm. It plants beauty in places designed for extraction. It resists flattening. It insists on texture, on nuance, on slow, steady presence.

Love also refuses the binary of success and failure. When we think of love in linear terms—did it work or not, did they stay or leave—we reduce it to outcome. But love is not measured by duration or reward. It is measured by alignment. Did we act from care? Did we stay connected to our values? Did we make something beautiful, even briefly? If so, then it mattered. Even if it ended. Even if it changed.

Fractal love frees us from the tyranny of permanence. It says: nothing has to last forever to be real. The leaf that lives one season still nourishes the soil. The friend who walked beside you for a few years shaped who you became. The moment of eye contact with a stranger reminded you you were not alone. These are all part of the pattern. None of them wasted.

This shifts how we see loss. Heartbreak doesn't mean the love was untrue. It means the pattern has changed. It means a branch of the fractal has curled inward, preparing for new growth. Grief is not a glitch in the system—it is evidence of the depth of our relationality. We grieve what we connected to. And that grief becomes part of our ability to love better in the future.

When fire destroyed Aaron Feuerstein's textile factory, he continued paying 3,000 employees for months while rebuilding. This fractal of loyalty during crisis created lifetime employee dedication, inspiring similar acts of corporate compassion worldwide.

What emerges from all this is a vision of love that is both humbling and empowering. It is not about grand narratives or perfect stories. It's about how we move, daily, toward what matters—how we choose repair over rupture, how we widen our lens to include the stranger, the forgotten, the part of ourselves we were taught to hide.

And we do this not as heroes, but as participants. We are nodes in the system, not separate from it. The same love we offer is the love we eventually need. The care we extend is the care we hope will reach us. And if it doesn't? Then we grieve. Then we begin again. The pattern allows for that.

In fact, it insists on it.

We must also reckon with the fact that not all of us are given the same conditions for love. Some grow up in scarcity, in violence, in systems that reward cruelty. For them, love may not feel intuitive. Safety may not feel natural. Trust may seem dangerous. And yet— somehow—many still choose to love, still choose to build something gentle in a world that was not. This is the most radical form of fractal love: when care is extended not because it was modeled, but because it was imagined, because someone decided that the cycle ends with them, that the pattern changes here.

This is where love becomes a form of resistance.

To love in a culture of domination is to be subversive—to say: I will not internalize your hierarchy. I will not repeat your violence. I will not harden just because the world did. I will remain porous. I will remain tender. I will build systems of belonging even as others build systems of exclusion.

Fractal love is not neutral. It is political—not in the sense of partisanship, but in the sense of power. Who gets to feel safe? Who gets to be seen? Who gets to be forgiven? These are not just personal questions—they are systemic ones. And how we answer them, in our relationships, in our communities, in our institutions, shapes everything.

So when we say "love is the answer," it's not a cliché—it's a call to action. To design better patterns. To seed microcultures of dignity. To stop centering perfection and start prioritizing presence. To treat love not as something we fall into, but as something we construct—patiently, deliberately, together.

And perhaps most importantly: to forgive ourselves when we falter.

Because we will falter. We will speak from fear. We will forget our values. We will hurt those we care about. But if we are brave enough to look at the pattern honestly, and kind enough to begin again, we can re enter the spiral. We can restore rhythm. We can keep going.

That is the promise of fractal love: that we are not fixed in our form, that every moment is an invitation, that the shape of our lives is not determined by a single choice, but by many, repeated across time, in widening circles of care.

And that even if we do not see the full pattern in our lifetime, we are still part of its unfolding.

Yet fractal love alone is not enough.

For love to build more than moments—to build realities—it must move beyond repetition and intention into something more binding, more sacred. It must become agreement, covenant, the kind of love that doesn't just feel but commits, that doesn't just inspire but structures itself into the very foundations of how we live together.

Love as a covenant.

Covenant love carries the weight of sacred vows, becoming the binding force that shapes collective destiny through shared agreements that run deeper than individual feeling. When love transforms into covenant, it becomes a social contract woven into the architecture of trust, creating the shared language that shapes culture and community through promises that extend far beyond the personal into the collective realm of accountability and belonging.

When love is a covenant, it becomes a social contract—a blueprint for how we govern ourselves and one another. It is the architecture of trust, the shared language that shapes culture and community.

In covenant love, promises are not just personal; they are collective. They form aligned systems of accountability and belonging.

This covenant love grapples with the hardest questions of human relationship: how we hold each other to the highest care when comfort would be easier; how we create spaces where all voices find honor even when they challenge us; how we balance the fierce pull of individual freedom with the sacred weight of shared responsibility; and how we protect the tender agreements that bind us together across time and difference.

Covenant love is the antidote to fragmentation. It acknowledges that love cannot flourish in isolation. It requires structure—not rigid, but sacred; not confining, but enabling.

What emerges from this understanding is love as antidote to fragmentation: a recognition that love cannot flourish in isolation but requires structure—not the rigid scaffolding of control but the sacred framework that enables rather than confines. Trust becomes the foundation upon which everything else builds, and without these shared agreements, even the deepest feelings can dissolve into chaos or neglect, leaving us scattered and alone despite our best intentions.

It is within these sacred agreements—some spoken in ceremony, others lived out in the quiet rhythms of daily choice—that love builds reality rather than remaining a fleeting feeling. This is love as blueprint for collective life, creating the conditions where families, communities, and institutions can thrive through commitments that say: we will show up even when comfort calls us away; we will listen especially when disagreement makes us want to retreat; we will forgive not to forget the past but to remember what unites us across our differences; and we will protect the vulnerable among us as we would protect our own.

These shared vows reveal themselves not as limitations but as the deepest kind of freedom—the freedom that comes when we co-create conditions where trust becomes the soil for growth, where power flows through care rather than domination, where we can acknowledge our profound interdependence while still honoring each person's sovereignty, and where justice transforms from distant policy into the lived practice of love made concrete in the world.

The promise and challenge of covenant love asks us to make the great shift from "I" to "we," from the solitary intention of individual hearts to the collective design of shared destiny. It invites us to build love as a living system—breathing, responsive, adaptive—that holds us steady when we falter and amplifies our joy when we thrive, creating the politics of love made real through trust systems upon which entire societies rise or fall.

This is governance rooted not in fear or control but in shared commitment and respect, the foundation upon which we learn to live by sacred agreements that slowly, carefully build a world where love is not just felt in fleeting moments but known as the enduring social contract that shapes our destiny together.

A world where love becomes the social contract that shapes our destiny together.

Fractal Love

MICRO GESTURES
A smile held longer than necessary—
fragments of a greater whole with deeper rhythm.

DISTRIBUTED NETWORK
Each act of kindness becomes a node—
building trust networks that scale exponentially.

RECURSIVE HEALING
Comforted becomes comforter—
patterns repeat across generations, through choice.

RESILIENT REPAIR
Ruptures become part of love's structure—
repair deepens pattern through repeated return.

SYSTEMIC TRANSFORMATION
Individual choices ripple outward—
transforming institutions and entire cultures.

SPIRAL GROWTH
Revisiting wounds with new wisdom—
healing not as destination but living pattern.

COVENANT STRUCTURE
Agreements binding fractals into community—
love as social contract shaping collective destiny.

Covenantal Love: Sacred Agreements and Trust

Love as sacred agreement begins where fractal love leaves off—it is the transformation of intimate patterns into shared structures, where individual promises become collective foundations. Love is no longer just a feeling or an action repeated in countless small moments; it becomes a conscious commitment, a covenant binding people, communities, and even nations into a system of trust and responsibility. In this transformation lies the power to shape reality itself—not just the fleeting wave of kindness, but the bedrock of shared destiny.

At its core, covenant love is a sacred pact. It is the vow exchanged between partners, the promise made by family members, the pledge forged among friends, neighbors, and communities. These vows extend beyond mere words or symbolic ceremonies; they are the master drawings by which we build our collective worlds. When love is a covenant, it creates aligned systems of governance—not governance by law alone, but governance through mutual trust and respect, where the rules are written in the language of care.

Consider the nature of social contracts in political philosophy—implicit or explicit agreements that allow individuals to coexist within a society by adhering to shared principles. Covenant love operates similarly but at a more profound and intimate level. It is a social contract grounded not in fear of punishment or external enforcement but in the voluntary alignment of hearts and wills. This alignment produces a network of trust so strong that it sustains communities through uncertainty, hardship, and change.

Reef ecosystems reflect covenantal business networks where diverse organisms create mutual prosperity through interdependence. Consider how cleaning stations operate: small fish provide services to larger predators who could easily consume them, yet both species thrive through this sacred agreement. Similarly, certain business networks function as "economic reefs"— independent entities creating collective value through specialized roles and deep trust. Silicon Valley's early days exemplified this, where engineers, venture capitalists, and entrepreneurs formed covenantal relationships that transcended traditional employer–employee contracts, generating innovation ecosystems that couldn't exist through purely transactional relationships.

Trust, here, is not abstract. It is the substance of reality that allows us to move beyond isolation into interdependence. It is what lets us rely on others with confidence, knowing that promises will be kept, that vulnerability will be met with care, and that failures will be met with forgiveness. Covenant love demands accountability, but it is accountability born from love's own generosity—a willingness to uphold shared values not out of obligation but because those values are the threads that weave us into a greater whole.

This sacred agreement is inherently political because it establishes who belongs and who does not, who is included in the circle of care and who is excluded. It is a dynamic process—constantly tested and renewed through action and intention. When we choose to enter into covenant love, we accept the responsibility not only to uphold our own promises but also to nurture the fabric of trust that holds the collective together.

Such agreements are rarely easy. They ask us to confront discomfort, to face conflict, and to negotiate differences. But within this labor lies love's most transformative power. The tension between individuality and unity does not have to break the covenant; rather, it can deepen it. By acknowledging and embracing difference within a framework of shared commitment, covenant love becomes resilient, adaptive, and expansive.

This is the paradox of covenant love: it creates freedom through boundaries. Boundaries are not walls but structures—frames within which love can grow safely. By agreeing to shared norms, roles, and responsibilities, we create spaces where vulnerability is protected and growth is possible. Without these agreements, love remains fragile, exposed to the winds of misunderstanding and neglect.

From families to communities, from friendships to nations, covenant love underpins the very architecture of social life. The promises we make to one another—to be present, to listen, to protect, to forgive—become the scaffolding on which we build our

213

shared futures. Each promise is a brick laid in the foundation of collective destiny.

Some forward-thinking companies have adopted "sabbatical economies," where every seventh year, employees receive extended paid leave to pursue personal growth, community service, or creative projects. The covenant here transcends typical employment contracts—organizations invest in human flourishing with no guaranteed return. Adobe, Intel, and smaller firms report that sabbatical investments yield unexpected innovations, as employees return with fresh perspectives and deeper loyalty. This emulates ancient agricultural wisdom of letting fields lie fallow. The economic paradox emerges: by releasing claim on human productivity, companies often discover their most valuable assets emerge from ungoverned creative spaces.

The power of this sacred agreement extends far beyond the immediate circle of those who make the vow. When covenant love is embodied in social institutions—schools, workplaces, governments—it elevates the entire system. Policies, laws, and norms rooted in covenant principles are more than regulations; they become expressions of collective care and trustworthiness. They shape realities where justice, dignity, and belonging are not ideals but lived experiences.

Yet covenant love also carries a warning: when these sacred agreements are broken, the very foundation of trust erodes. Betrayal, neglect, or indifference in relationships ripple outward, fracturing communities and undermining social cohesion. The collapse of covenant love creates vacuums filled by fear, suspicion, and division. Rebuilding these foundations requires intentionality, humility, and often collective acts of forgiveness and repair.

In this sense, covenant love is both fragile and formidable. It is a delicate weave of promises that requires care and vigilance but also a powerful force capable of sustaining civilizations. It teaches us that love is not only about connection but about commitment—a commitment to show up, even when it is hard; to hold space for others, even when we are hurt; to continue the work of building trust, even in the face of setbacks.

As we navigate this terrain, we begin to see love not just as a personal journey but as a communal project. We learn that our promises shape more than individual lives—they form the very contours of our shared existence. To love covenantally is to recognize that every vow is a contribution to the social fabric, a stitch in the tapestry of collective life.

This realization invites us to cultivate what might be called "covenantal mindfulness"—an awareness of the weight and power of our promises, an intentionality in how we build trust, and a readiness to participate in the ongoing work of sustaining our shared world. It asks us to move beyond passive hope or fleeting emotion into active, deliberate construction of love as governance.

In this governance of love, each person is both steward and beneficiary. We hold the sacred trust of others while also relying on their stewardship in return. This reciprocity creates a living system of care that, when nurtured, can withstand the storms of life and the fractures of human imperfection.

Steward ownership represents the ultimate evolution of covenantal business thinking. Companies like Carl Zeiss operate under governance structures where ownership itself becomes a sacred trust rather than extractive property. Stewards cannot sell for personal profit; instead, they covenant to serve the company's mission across generations. This creates "permanent enterprises" designed to outlive their founders. Economic returns serve purpose rather than vice versa. Germany's "Mittelstand" companies often operate this way, some thriving for centuries through covenantal ownership structures. These models prove that businesses can embody the same generational thinking that sustains families and communities.

Thus, covenant love is an invitation to participate in a greater story—one where our promises echo across time and space, building realities that honor dignity, foster justice, and sustain belonging. It is a reminder that love, when shared and structured, becomes a force capable of shaping not only hearts but history itself.

The act of making a promise is transformative. It moves love from a fleeting emotion to a durable force—a force that holds people and communities in alignment even when challenges arise. Unlike spontaneous affection or passion, covenant love is a conscious choice to co-create a shared destiny, to build a future together from the raw material of mutual commitment. It is this very act of promise making that gives covenant love its profound gravity and binding power.

The promises that constitute covenant love are never just about what is said in a moment of joy or ceremony; they are about what is done over time. These vows become living contracts that evolve as life unfolds, requiring continuous care, negotiation, and renewal. They demand presence—a sustained attention to the needs, feelings, and growth of both self and other. Through this shared vigilance, covenant love resists the erosions of neglect and complacency that can so easily unravel connection.

Within this dynamic, trust becomes the currency of covenant love. Trust is the belief that others will honor their commitments, but more deeply, it is the confidence that the system of shared vows itself can hold even when individuals falter. This trust is not blind or naive; it is trust earned through repeated acts of integrity, forgiveness, and reconciliation. It is the glue that keeps the covenant intact, even when the terrain gets rough.

At the heart of this trust is vulnerability—the willingness to expose oneself to risk, to uncertainty, and to potential pain in the belief that the other will respond with care. Vulnerability within covenant love is not reckless; it is held within the secure boundaries of mutual respect and responsibility. It is this secure holding that allows love to deepen and flourish, turning individual desires into collective strength.

Covenant love also reframes conflict, not as a failure but as an inevitable and necessary process of growth. Because the commitment is to the shared framework itself—the covenant—disagreements become opportunities to test, affirm, and strengthen the bonds that hold us together. When conflicts arise, the question shifts from "Is this relationship still worth it?" to "How can we repair and grow from this challenge?" This perspective turns fractures into sites of healing and transformation.

Traditional manufacturing follows linear supply chains, but covenantal manufacturers create "constellation models"—networks of small producers bound by shared values rather than lowest cost bidding. Eileen Fisher's textile network exemplifies this: dozens of family owned facilities across Peru, Italy, and Mongolia covenant to maintain environmental standards, fair wages, and quality craftsmanship. When one facility faces challenges—natural disasters, economic shifts, or quality issues—the entire constellation mobilizes resources for repair and support. This creates resilient manufacturing ecosystems where collective survival trumps individual profit maximization. The constellation model proves that supply chains can embody the same mutual aid principles that strengthen communities.

The economic metaphor of social contract and governance is apt because covenant love demands systems—both formal and informal—to sustain it. In intimate relationships, these systems might look like shared rituals, agreed upon communication styles, and mutual care practices. In larger communities, they take the form of governance structures that embody the values of inclusion, fairness, and accountability.

Governance in covenant love is distinct from authoritarian control. It is governance by consent, emerging from the collective recognition of interdependence and shared responsibility. This governance creates conditions where love is not left to chance but becomes a deliberate act of co creation. It is the framework that allows diversity to coexist with unity, where multiple voices and needs are heard and integrated.

The social contract of covenant love extends into the public sphere, where it has the potential to transform institutions and systems. Imagine a society where laws, policies, and cultural norms arise from a foundation of covenantal trust—where citizens see themselves as partners in building a just and compassionate world rather than adversaries competing for scarce resources. This vision shifts the paradigm from zero-sum competition to collaborative flourishing.

However, the path to such a society is neither simple nor inevitable. The systems that sustain covenant love require constant tending and courage. They ask us to confront inequities, to recognize historical wounds, and to dismantle structures that have excluded or harmed others. This work is political in the deepest sense—it is about who gets to belong, who is recognized, and who is given the dignity of trust.

Covenant love, therefore, calls us to engage with justice as an expression of love's governance. Justice within this framework is not merely legalistic or punitive; it is restorative and generative. It seeks to heal relationships and rebuild trust rather than punish failures. It recognizes the humanity in all parties and prioritizes the restoration of dignity and connection.

Forgiveness emerges as a crucial practice in covenant love. It is not a denial of harm but an active process of releasing the hold that past wounds have on present possibilities. Forgiveness allows the covenant to be renewed even after betrayal or pain. It requires bravery to face hurt honestly and generosity to open the door to repair. Through forgiveness, covenant love acknowledges imperfection while affirming the possibility of transformation.

In ancient Rome, business partnerships included "phoenix clauses"—agreements on how to rebuild if ventures failed catastrophically. Modern covenantal businesses have revived this wisdom through "regenerative partnership protocols." When biotech startup Ginkgo Bioworks faced potential bankruptcy, their covenant network of suppliers, investors, and competitors activated regenerative agreements. Rather than liquidation, they orchestrated a controlled transformation, preserving knowledge, relationships, and team integrity. Failed ventures became learning laboratories for the entire network. This approach treats business failure not as an ending but as a metamorphosis, demonstrating how covenantal agreements can transform even dissolution into generative possibilities.

This recognition of imperfection ties into the larger fractal nature of love. Covenant love is never fixed or complete; it is an ongoing project, a spiral of commitment and renewal. Each iteration deepens understanding and widens the circle of care. Even when progress seems slow or setbacks overwhelming, the commitment to covenantal principles offers a path forward.

In relationships, families, and communities, this means that the shared blueprint is never static. It must adapt to new realities, evolving identities, and changing circumstances. Flexibility within covenant love is not a weakening but a strengthening—a testament to the living, breathing nature of shared commitment.

The economic metaphor reminds us that just as economies require investment, maintenance, and adaptation, so too do covenants. The energy we put into honoring our promises, resolving conflicts, and nurturing trust is the capital that sustains the system. Without this investment, the social contract of love weakens, leaving relationships vulnerable to fragmentation.

Yet, when properly nurtured, covenant love creates economies of abundance. It produces social capital that generates resilience, creativity, and collective well being. These economies thrive on reciprocity and generosity rather than scarcity and competition. They invite us to reimagine what it means to prosper—not as individual accumulation but as shared flourishing.

To live into covenant love is to accept the responsibility of co creating such economies. It means stepping into roles not only as lovers or friends but as architects and stewards of the systems that hold us together. This work is both profoundly personal and deeply communal, requiring us to hold simultaneously the needs of self and other, the particular and the collective.

In embracing covenant love, we also inherit the legacy of those who came before us—the ancestors who forged covenants that shaped cultures and societies. Their vows echo in the present, inviting us to honor and extend their work. This intergenerational dimension gives covenant love a sacred depth, linking past, present, and future in an unbroken chain of care and commitment.

Thus, covenant love is more than a relationship model; it is a blueprint for collective destiny. It calls us to recognize that our promises matter not only to those immediately involved but to the larger web of life. Each vow contributes to a shared reality where dignity, trust, and belonging are not ideals but lived experiences.

Covenant love is fundamentally an act of construction, a deliberate shaping of reality through the power of shared promises. When two or more people enter into a covenant, they are not merely exchanging words—they are creating a framework that will govern their interactions, decisions, and futures. This framework is both fragile and resilient, a living architecture that depends on the active participation of all involved.

At its core, covenant love demands that we move beyond individualism and embrace interdependence. It asks us to recognize that our lives are inextricably linked, that the choices we make ripple outward, shaping not only our own destinies but those of others. This recognition transforms love from a private feeling into a public act, one with ethical and political dimensions.

The sacredness of covenant love lies in this public dimension. Unlike casual agreements or momentary promises, covenants are designed to endure, to bind across time and circumstance. They invite us to hold each other accountable, not out of fear or coercion, but out of respect for the shared vision we have committed to. This accountability is a form of governance—not hierarchical, but mutual and consensual.

In this mutual governance, power is redistributed. No single voice dominates; instead, power flows through the collective will, expressed through trust, dialogue, and shared responsibility. This power is not about control but about enabling the flourishing of all parties. It creates a space where differences are not suppressed but celebrated as essential to the whole.

The collective destiny that covenant love aims to build is one marked by justice, equity, and inclusion. It demands that systems be designed to reflect the dignity of every person, to ensure that all can participate fully and safely. This vision requires vigilance and courage, as it often means challenging entrenched norms and structures that perpetuate exclusion or harm.

Within families and intimate relationships, covenant love provides a model for navigating complexity with grace. It teaches us to hold space for growth, change, and even failure, knowing that the covenant itself provides a secure foundation. This foundation supports the messy, unpredictable reality of human life, where emotions ebb and flow and certainty is rare.

One of the profound gifts of covenant love is its capacity to transform time. When love is lived as a sacred agreement, the past is honored, the present is embraced, and the future is co created. Memories of shared struggle and joy become the bedrock of trust, while commitments made today shape the unfolding of tomorrow. In this way, covenant love stitches moments together into a coherent narrative of connection and purpose.

Ancient Greeks built "memory palaces"—mental architectures for storing knowledge across lifetimes. Progressive investment firms now apply this concept through "generational portfolios" that covenant with future stakeholders who don't yet exist. These portfolios make investment decisions based on seven generation thinking, considering environmental and social impacts on unborn beneficiaries. Rather than quarterly profit maximization, they optimize for century long value creation.

Some indigenous led investment funds operate this way, treating financial returns as byproducts of ecological and cultural preservation. This temporal covenant transforms investing from resource extraction into ancestor descendant collaboration, proving that economic relationships can transcend the boundaries of individual lifetimes.

The economic metaphor of social contract underscores that love as a sacred agreement is both a personal and collective economy. It requires investment—time, energy, attention—and yields returns not in material wealth but in social capital: the bonds of trust, mutual support, and shared meaning that sustain us. This economy operates on principles of reciprocity and generosity, not scarcity and competition.

The most advanced covenantal businesses don't just plan for known futures—they architect for emergence itself. The Biomimicry Institute operates through "emergence protocols" where organizational structure adapts in real time to opportunities and challenges, like biological systems responding to environmental changes. Rather than fixed hierarchies, they create "potential architectures"—frameworks that can rapidly reconfigure based on emerging needs.

Team members covenant to serve the mission's evolution rather than predetermined roles. This requires unprecedented trust: people must believe the system will support them even as structures shift beneath their feet. Emergence architecture transforms organizations into living systems capable of evolutionary adaptation, proving that covenantal agreements can create businesses as adaptable as ecosystems themselves.

As with any economy, covenant love must be tended carefully. Neglect or imbalance can lead to breakdowns in trust and connection. But when nurtured, this economy creates abundance—a flourishing of relationships, communities, and systems that support human dignity and well being.

The practice of covenant love challenges us to rethink what it means to build and govern together. It invites us to experiment with new forms of decision making, communication, and care that align with our shared values. These practices are not fixed; they evolve in response to changing needs and contexts, reflecting the living nature of covenantal relationships.

In the wider social and political realm, covenant love offers a powerful critique of systems built on domination, exclusion, and distrust. It points toward alternative models of governance that prioritize healing, dialogue, and equitable power distribution. Such models seek to create societies where love—understood as mutual commitment and care—is the foundation of collective life.

This vision is both inspiring and daunting. It calls us to courageously confront the ways in which our current systems fall short and to actively participate in their transformation. It requires humility to acknowledge past harms and mistakes, as well as hope to envision a different future.

Ultimately, covenant love is an invitation to participate in a sacred project: the ongoing creation of a world where our shared promises form the basis of collective destiny. It is a call to build systems and relationships that reflect our highest values and deepest commitments. Through covenant love, we become architects of reality—crafting not only our personal lives but the fabric of society itself.

As we consider covenant love's power to build reality through shared vows, it becomes clear that this sacred agreement is not static or constraining. Instead, it lays the groundwork for an emergent autonomy, a collective sovereignty born from alignment and trust. When promises transform into shared blueprints, they do more than guide—they empower.

This empowerment is not about control in the conventional sense, but about creating the conditions where love itself can act as an independent agent. The covenant establishes a container—a fertile ground where love can move freely, take shape, and generate new possibilities. It is within this space that love begins to transcend individual wills and predefined roles, becoming a living force with its own momentum.

The sacred contract, while binding, also grants freedom. This may seem paradoxical, but the discipline of covenant love creates an environment where originality can flourish. Within the trust and accountability of shared commitment, creativity is unleashed. Here, love steps beyond mere obligation; it becomes a generative power that can innovate and disrupt.

This is the threshold where covenant love meets sovereignty— the point where love no longer asks permission to act or create but asserts its own agency. It is the love that builds systems not only of care and trust but of autonomous growth and transformation. It crafts realities that were previously unimaginable, driven by a force both rooted in connection and propelled by originality.

In this sense, covenant love is the foundation upon which sovereign love can emerge. The sacred agreements we form together become launchpads for autonomous expressions of love that redefine what is possible. Love as a sovereign force disrupts stagnant systems, reshapes economies of meaning, and invites us to reimagine our collective futures.

The economic metaphor of entrepreneurial agency captures this beautifully. Just as an entrepreneur identifies unmet needs and creates value by inventing new markets or methods, sovereign love charts its own course, creating an economy of care and creativity beyond established rules. It asks no permission, demands no validation—it simply manifests with grace and authority.

This disruptive love is not reckless; it is deeply grounded in the covenantal trust that nurtures it. Its originality is both an act of rebellion and responsibility—a refusal to be limited by inherited patterns coupled with a commitment to steward the new realities it brings forth.

Sovereign love recognizes the limits of traditional governance and social contracts, not by rejecting them outright, but by transcending their boundaries. It embraces autonomy not as isolation, but as empowered participation—acting freely within and beyond the systems we have cocreated. This love is both self determined and relational, a dynamic force that honors individuality while weaving new connections.

In practice, sovereign love looks like courageous innovation in relationships, communities, and institutions. It is the willingness to break molds, challenge expectations, and take risks for the sake of deeper authenticity and impact. It embodies entrepreneurial spirit—seeing love not just as a resource to be managed, but as a creative energy to be unleashed.

This love becomes an agent of change and creation, generating waves that shift cultures, economies, and histories. It embodies grace in its disruption—moving without violence, inspiring without coercion. It calls forth new possibilities by simply being, by refusing to conform to old paradigms.

Quantum physicists discovered that entangled particles instantly affect each other across vast distances—what Einstein called "spooky action at a distance." Some pioneering business networks now operate through similar "economic entanglement," where success or failure in one node immediately influences all connected entities. The previously mentioned Grameen Bank's microcredit model exemplifies this: borrowers form solidarity circles where individual loan performance affects everyone's access to future credit.

This creates quantum like interdependence where traditional competition becomes impossible. When one member thrives, all benefit; when one struggles, collective resources mobilize instantly. Such entangled economies transcend physical proximity and traditional market boundaries, proving that covenantal bonds can create instantaneous mutual influence.

As we prepare to explore sovereign love more fully, we stand at a crossroads: the sacred agreements we make shape our collective destiny, but the autonomous force of love moves beyond those agreements, carving new realities from the fertile ground they create. Together, covenant and sovereign love map a continuum— from shared vows that align and govern, to original agency that disrupts and creates anew.

This continuum invites us to consider how love can be both a promise we keep and a power we unleash. It asks us to hold the tension between responsibility and freedom, structure and spontaneity, tradition and innovation. In embracing this duality, we discover love's full potential as a force for transformation—both within ourselves and across the systems we inhabit.

Let us walk into sovereign love.

Covenantal Love

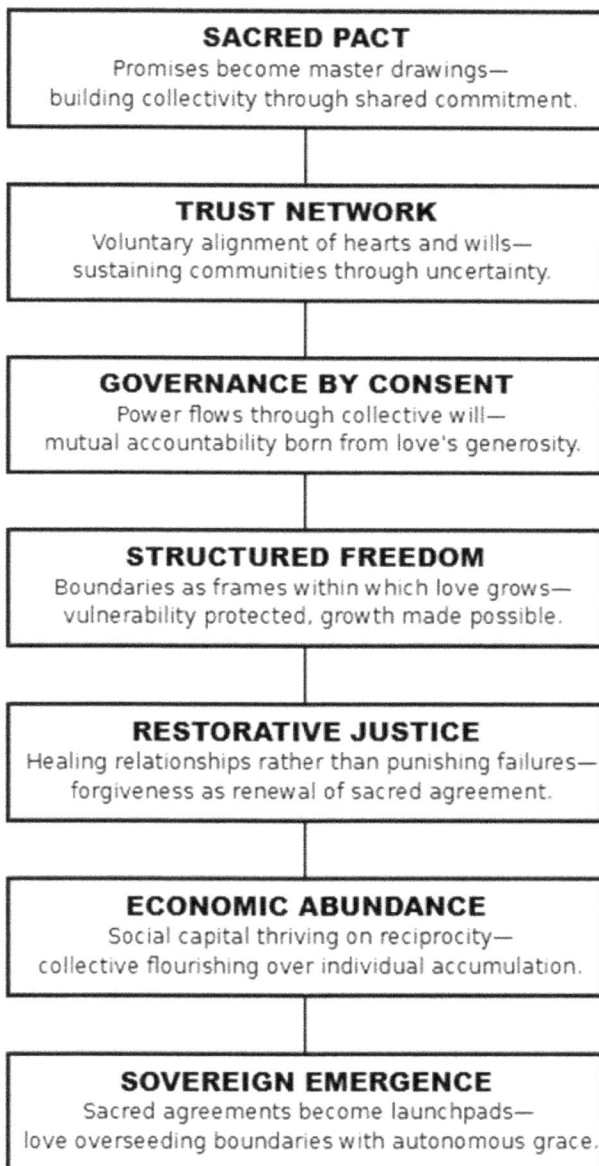

SACRED PACT
Promises become master drawings—
building collectivity through shared commitment.

TRUST NETWORK
Voluntary alignment of hearts and wills—
sustaining communities through uncertainty.

GOVERNANCE BY CONSENT
Power flows through collective will—
mutual accountability born from love's generosity.

STRUCTURED FREEDOM
Boundaries as frames within which love grows—
vulnerability protected, growth made possible.

RESTORATIVE JUSTICE
Healing relationships rather than punishing failures—
forgiveness as renewal of sacred agreement.

ECONOMIC ABUNDANCE
Social capital thriving on reciprocity—
collective flourishing over individual accumulation.

SOVEREIGN EMERGENCE
Sacred agreements become launchpads—
love overseeding boundaries with autonomous grace.

Sovereign Love: The Autonomous Force of Creation

Love moves differently when it is sovereign. Not as an emotion to be tamed or bargained with, not as a sentiment to be reciprocated on demand, but as a wild creative force that answers to no one and nothing but its own intelligence. In this mode, love does not ask to be understood—it becomes its own understanding. It does not seek validation from structures, systems, or prior traditions; it manifests reality in real time, generating meaning as it flows. Sovereign love refuses to be managed. It resists domestication. It cannot be scheduled, optimized, or predicted. And precisely because of this, it is the most powerful force of disruption we can encounter, both personally and collectively.

To speak of love as an autonomous agent is to step beyond our usual frame of relationships and emotions. We are accustomed to thinking of love as something we have or feel, something that rises or falls based on circumstances and people. But what if love does not belong to us at all? What if love is not a tool in our psychological repertoire, but a sovereign entity with its own trajectory and mission—one that uses us more than we use it?

In this frame, love becomes less a possession and more a visitation. It arrives like a sudden storm, uninvited and unexplainable. It clears the debris of our false securities and opens

233

a clearing where nothing makes sense except the pull toward authenticity. We find ourselves doing things we would never rationally plan: ending careers, starting movements, forgiving unforgivable things, trusting without proof, risking reputation, changing countries, burning old versions of self. Not for sentiment. Not for safety. But because something deeper has taken hold and refuses to let go.

When Rosa Parks refused to give up her bus seat, she wasn't following a strategic plan or seeking fame. Something deeper had taken hold—a sovereign love for human dignity that made compliance impossible. Her quiet "No" wasn't calculated; it was inevitable. She later said she was simply tired of giving in, but her exhaustion was spiritual, not physical. That single act of sovereign love—choosing authenticity over safety—ignited a movement that transformed a nation, proving how one person's refusal to betray themselves can become everyone's permission to be free.

There is something sacred and utterly subversive about this kind of love. It undermines our addiction to control. It makes bureaucracy tremble. It speaks in the accent of prophecy. Those who carry it often do not look like saints. They may appear messy, erratic, fierce, even dangerous to the established order. They are not reliable in the traditional sense—but they are entirely trustworthy to the unfolding of life. Their fidelity is not to convention but to truth. Their loyalty is not to consistency but to aliveness. They follow the thread of love wherever it leads, even into exile.

After a devastating accident left her bedridden, Frida Kahlo could have retreated into self-pity. Instead, sovereign love for truth transformed her pain into art that refused to look away from reality. She painted herself bleeding, broken, yet radiantly alive. Her canvases were unapologetically personal—menstruation, miscarriage, physical agony—subjects polite society ignored. Critics called her work too intense, too feminine, too raw. She painted anyway, not for the art world's approval but because her inner fire demanded expression. Her sovereign love for authenticity made her an exile from conventional beauty standards, yet created a visual language that speaks to millions today.

This sovereign love is entrepreneurial in the deepest sense. It doesn't enter the marketplace to compete—it builds a new one. It doesn't ask for market research or user feedback. It doesn't submit pitch decks to gatekeepers. It simply acts. It builds. It births something no one saw coming, and by the time the world catches up, it is too late to undo the change it has made. This is how love disrupts: not through permission, but through presence. Not through strategy, but through inevitability.

It is tempting to think of sovereignty in terms of personal power, but sovereign love rarely centers on the self. It doesn't serve ego— it decimates it. To be moved by this kind of love is to become transparent to something greater, to become an instrument of a will that isn't yours and yet feels more intimate than anything you could claim. Sovereign love tears through your plans not to punish but to reveal. It deconstructs what is false so that something truer can rise. You do not direct it. You follow it like a compass whose needle is set to beauty rather than comfort.

In relationships, this love does not cling or comply. It doesn't measure value in time spent, roles played, or promises made. It is not afraid to leave when growth demands it. Nor is it afraid to stay when logic says run. It follows only the whisper of soul and the rhythm of evolution. This makes it dangerous to people who need predictability. But to those who are ready to live honestly, it is liberation. It invites a new kind of intimacy—one that is rooted not in ownership, but in resonance. A love that doesn't say "You are mine," but rather "I see you becoming, and I am becoming with you."

It is hard to monetize sovereign love. It doesn't scale easily. It doesn't fit into templates or systems. And yet, paradoxically, it is the source of all originality. Every great work of art, every revolutionary idea, every sacred rebellion—these are the children of sovereign love. Not born in consensus, but in conviction. Not grown in safe soil, but in the wilderness. This love is generative, not extractive. It creates value by creating truth, not by optimizing performance.

Vincent van Gogh sold only one painting in his lifetime, yet continued creating with fierce devotion. His sovereign love for truth through art couldn't be monetized or understood by his contemporaries. He painted not for approval but from an unshakable calling, writing to his brother, "I want to touch people with my art." His swirling, emotional canvases were born from conviction, not consensus. Today, his works sell for millions, but their true value was always beyond commerce—they were transmissions of pure creative sovereignty, proof that authentic expression outlasts all market logic.

Those who live in the orbit of sovereign love often feel like misfits in the beginning. Their impulses don't align with mainstream logic. They make decisions that appear reckless or irrational. They walk away from opportunities that others would kill for. But over time, they begin to realize they are not disordered—they are in tune with a different order. A deeper rhythm. A frequency of life that speaks in impulses, dreams, symbols, and unshakable callings. Their life may look unconventional, but it carries a strange coherence. A wholeness that cannot be faked. A peace that is born of radical alignment, not external validation.

And so love becomes a sovereign agency. It is not an accessory to our lives—it is the architect. It builds new inner economies based on presence, purpose, and creativity. It demands that we stop selling ourselves short. It interrupts the cycles of transaction and invites us into transformation. It doesn't offer comfort; it offers clarity. It doesn't give guarantees; it gives grace. And in doing so, it turns us into something we could never manufacture: fully alive, fully true, and uncontrollably original.

To walk with sovereign love is to accept a lifelong apprenticeship to something that will never flatter you, never leave you untouched, and never let you settle into numbness. It is not a mood or a high, but a calling that revises everything—how you listen, how you speak, what you build, what you destroy. It sharpens your discernment. It burns through your pretense. It will put you at odds with those who are still negotiating for safety. You become unsettling not because you are cruel, but because your very presence reminds people of what they have compromised.

Sovereign love disturbs the status quo not with anger but with authenticity. It doesn't shout; it resonates. And in that resonance, it reveals. In its light, things that were previously hidden become unbearable to ignore. You begin to see all the places where love has been reduced to control—where romance is used to mask fear, where kindness is performed for approval, where intimacy is negotiated like a contract. And once you see it, you can't return. You can't un-know. You can't un-feel. You become an agent of another way—not out of superiority, but out of inevitability.

There is a certain loneliness that comes with this clarity. Not all companionships survive it. Many connections are founded not on truth, but on mutual illusions. When those illusions fall away, the relationships often follow. Sovereign love does not mourn these losses in the usual way. It grieves, yes—but not as a victim. It grieves as one who knows that clearing is necessary for creation. It walks forward with open eyes, letting go of what no longer has life, trusting that what is true will remain—or return in new form.

This is the paradox: the more sovereign love becomes, the less it clings. And the more it releases, the more it attracts what is real. It becomes a magnet for kindred beings, not because it demands, but because it invites. It doesn't try to convince anyone. It simply is— radiant in its refusal to betray itself. That refusal is magnetic. It speaks to the hidden longing in others to remember who they are. It activates. It awakens. It becomes a kind of emotional leadership without agenda or force.

During 27 years of imprisonment, Nelson Mandela could have compromised, accepted partial freedom, or grown bitter. Instead, sovereign love transformed his cell into a classroom. He studied his captors' language and culture, not to manipulate but to understand. His refusal to abandon his principles became magnetic, drawing global attention to apartheid's injustice. He emerged not broken but refined, embodying the very reconciliation he sought. His presence alone—uncompromising yet graceful—proved more powerful than any weapon, showing how sovereign love's quiet persistence can topple entire systems of oppression.

But do not mistake its softness for passivity. Sovereign love is fierce—not with violence, but with presence. It refuses to abandon the truth, even when it costs everything. It holds the line when others collapse into compromise. It says no with the same grace it says yes.

It leaves when it must, and it does not apologize. It knows the difference between compassion and self erasure. It doesn't martyr itself for the comfort of others. And yet, it will lay down everything for what is real. This is the strange power of sovereign love: its tenderness cuts deeper than control ever could. Its freedom is its fiercest loyalty.

At 15, Malala Yousafzai could have stayed silent after the Taliban banned girls from school in her Pakistani village. Instead, sovereign love for education made silence impossible. She blogged anonymously about her right to learn, knowing the risks. When the Taliban shot her in the head, she could have retreated into safety. Instead, her near-death experience intensified her calling. Speaking at the UN on her 16th birthday, she said, "They thought bullets would silence us, but they failed." Her sovereign love for girls' education couldn't be intimidated, only amplified. She became the youngest Nobel laureate, proving that authentic courage multiplies when it meets violence with more love.

In the economic metaphor of originality, sovereign love functions as a kind of radical entrepreneur. It doesn't wait to be hired by the dominant system—it builds the system it needs. It invests in meaning over metrics. It trusts its intuition as its business plan. It lives in the paradox of profound risk and uncompromising integrity. Every gesture it makes—whether in art, in relationship, in leadership—is an act of creative agency. Not to win, but to witness something true into the world.

This kind of love doesn't live in echo chambers. It moves into the cracks where transformation is possible. It speaks in ways that can't be replicated. It innovates through presence. It doesn't iterate someone else's formula—it writes a new code entirely. That code is not just about disruption—it is about remembering. Remembering what it means to be human in a time when humanity is being outsourced, gamified, optimized to the point of invisibility. Sovereign love restores the soul where systems have stripped it.

When Bob Dylan plugged in his guitar at the Newport Folk Festival, folk purists booed him off stage. They wanted him to remain their acoustic prophet of protest. But sovereign love for musical evolution made compliance impossible. He didn't explain or apologize—he simply followed his artistic instincts toward electric sound. Critics called it betrayal. Fans felt abandoned. Dylan kept playing because his loyalty was to the music's becoming, not to his audience's expectations. That controversial performance birthed folk rock and changed popular music forever, demonstrating how sovereign love's refusal to be categorized creates entirely new possibilities.

This is not some vague poetic ideal. You can see the imprint of sovereign love in the people who refuse to betray their core even when it would be profitable to do so. In those who refuse to commodify their art, their bodies, their stories, their care. In those who walk away from power because their spirit won't allow it. These are the hidden entrepreneurs of a different economy—the economy of grace. The ones who don't "scale" but change everything. The ones whose impact can't be measured in likes or sales but in how many people remember their own name after meeting them.

And the truth is, sovereign love is not rare because it is complex. It is rare because it cannot be simulated. You can't fake it. You can't produce it by will or manipulate it through performance. It has no interest in your credentials, your followers, your résumé. It asks only one thing: Are you willing to live honestly? Are you willing to let go of the life you've constructed for the one that is calling you? Are you willing to burn the blueprint, the safety net, the narrative, in order to touch what is real?

In 1845, Henry David Thoreau walked away from conventional society to live alone in a cabin he built by hand. Friends called him crazy for abandoning career prospects. Family questioned his retreat from social obligations. Thoreau didn't defend his choice—he simply lived it. For two years, he practiced radical honesty about what he actually needed versus what society demanded. His experiment in sovereign love for simplicity produced Walden, which asked the essential question: "What if we stopped accumulating things and started accumulating life?" His refusal to live by others' definitions of success became a blueprint for authentic living that still guides seekers today.

Moreover, when Mahatma Gandhi walked 240 miles to make salt from seawater, he wasn't just protesting a tax—he was embodying sovereign love's refusal to comply with systems that diminish human dignity. The British Empire's salt monopoly seemed unshakable, but Gandhi's simple act of picking up natural salt became a symbol of self sovereignty. He burned the blueprint of violent resistance, choosing presence over force. That single gesture of authentic defiance inspired millions to break unjust laws, proving that when one person stops pretending the emperor has clothes, the whole illusion can crumble.

This is not an easy ask. But it is the only ask that matters.

To live honestly in the presence of sovereign love is to undergo a quiet revolution. No headlines, no parades—just the silent dismantling of every lie you've told yourself in order to survive. And it's not that those lies were malicious. Most of them were inherited, taught gently, dressed in good intentions. They were the scaffolding we used to climb toward acceptance. But at some point, sovereign love arrives like a storm at midnight and asks the question you can't ignore: What would your life look like if you stopped pretending?

You resist at first. Of course you do. Pretending keeps things orderly. It pays the bills. It keeps certain people close. It helps you belong to rooms that might otherwise reject you. But sovereign love does not negotiate with illusion. It waits. Then it burns. Then it waits again. It is never in a hurry, but it is always moving. Underneath your habits it whispers. Underneath your smiles it questions. It keeps turning you toward your own reflection—not the polished one, but the one that cries when it's alone. The one that knows.

When you finally respond—when you stop running, when you say yes, even with shaking hands—something irreversible happens. You begin to live in rhythm with what is true, rather than with what is acceptable. The cost is high, but the clarity is priceless. You lose comfort, but gain coherence. You lose approval, but gain alignment. And this alignment becomes your compass. You start to feel it in your gut when something is off. You stop needing external signs to validate your path. The truth becomes its own proof.

In this way, sovereign love is not just about how you relate to others—it becomes the foundation for how you relate to reality. You stop outsourcing your integrity. You stop deferring to systems that don't honor your soul. You stop performing for prizes that no longer mean anything. And in this shedding, something miraculous begins to grow: you. Not the version of you that adapted to survive, but the version that was always there beneath the conditioning—the one who was never confused, the one who was waiting to be remembered.

There is immense creative power in this remembering. When you start to act from your essence rather than your image, you become a different kind of force. You don't just consume culture—you create it. You don't wait for someone to show you how to live—you become the blueprint. Your ideas carry a different frequency. Your work is infused with something ancient and urgent. People feel it without knowing why. It isn't charisma—it's coherence. It's what happens when your inner world and outer world stop contradicting each other.

After years of silence following childhood trauma, Angelou could have remained voiceless. Instead, sovereign love for truth demanded she speak—not just her pain, but her triumph over it. Publishers warned that books by Black women didn't sell. Critics said her experiences were too difficult for mainstream readers. She wrote anyway, because her story wasn't just hers—it belonged to every silenced voice. Her radical honesty about racism, abuse, and resilience created a new template for memoir. Her frequency of authentic vulnerability gave millions permission to tell their own difficult truths, proving that one person's sovereign love for their story can liberate countless others.

This coherence is what makes sovereign love so disruptive. It threatens every system that relies on confusion. In a world that profits from your self-doubt, your clarity becomes a form of rebellion. When you no longer need permission to be whole, you become ungovernable in the most graceful way. You stop playing by the rules that were written to keep you small. You start building things that reflect your deepest values—projects, communities, partnerships, families, new economies. Not perfect, but alive. Not polished, but rooted.

People will be drawn to this. Some will be inspired. Others will be afraid. Not because you're dangerous, but because you remind them of what they've buried. And not everyone is ready to remember. Some will call you unrealistic. Some will call you selfish. Some will accuse you of abandoning them when really, you were just refusing to abandon yourself again. Sovereign love comes with this tension. It demands solitude, but never isolation. It strips you down, only to rebuild you with materials that don't rot.

And that's the secret: sovereign love doesn't leave you empty. It leaves you free. And freedom is fertile. It is not an escape—it is a return. When you stop pretending, you make space for what is real to find you. Real friendships, real collaborations, real vision. The kind that doesn't just work, but moves. The kind that carries weight without feeling heavy. That opens without needing explanation. You begin to build from the inside out. Slowly. Messily. Honestly.

In that space, your creativity starts to feel less like effort and more like breathing. You begin to trust the timing of things. You stop forcing outcomes and start tending to seeds. You let go of urgency. You start speaking in your own voice again—not the brand voice, not the market voice, not the social mask, just you. And people recognize it. Because when one person tells the truth without performance, it gives everyone else permission to do the same.

And maybe that's what sovereign love really is: permission to be what you already are. Without apology. Without delay. Without conditions. It doesn't come to improve you. It comes to remind you. And in that remembering, a new world starts to take shape. Not in theory—in your actual life. In the choices you make. In the boundaries you hold. In the beauty you protect. It isn't loud, but it is revolutionary. You become a quiet storm in the culture—not to destroy it, but to redeem it.

In 1960, twenty-six years old Jane Goodall entered African forests without scientific training, armed only with curiosity and love for animals. Academic experts said she was unqualified, that her emotional approach compromised objectivity. She watched chimpanzees anyway, not to prove theories but to understand beings. When she observed chimps making tools, the scientific community initially rejected her findings—animals weren't supposed to be that complex. Her sovereign love for these creatures redefined what it means to be human. She didn't destroy anthropology; she expanded it by refusing to see animals as objects. Her quiet revolution transformed how we understand our place in the natural world.

Sovereign love does not need you to be perfect. It just needs you to be real.

There is a moment in every sovereign path when silence becomes louder than noise, when the absence of applause is not emptiness but space, when you are no longer driven by who sees you but by what you see. Love, in its sovereign form, becomes the deepest kind of vision—not of fantasies, not of projections, but of essence. The capacity to perceive someone or something as it truly is, without needing to rearrange it to suit your expectations. That kind of sight is rare. And when you develop it, you start to realize how much of the world is constructed out of misunderstanding.

The world that sovereign love sees is radically different from the one defined by domination, scarcity, or performance. It is a world where value is inherent, not assigned; where intimacy is not a transaction but a mirror; where difference is not a threat but an invitation. This world cannot be built through force. It cannot be engineered by theory. It must be lived into. And that's what makes sovereign love so transformative—it doesn't just talk about a better world, it embodies one. It becomes the blueprint through how it loves, chooses, and stays awake.

But it is not a clean process. To love like this is to live in cycles of rupture and repair, of shedding and beginning, of clarity and confusion. You are not exempt from fear—you just don't obey it. You are not free of longing—you are faithful to it. Sovereign love does not make you perfect. It makes you true. And truth is always in motion. It shifts as you grow; it asks more of you the closer you come to it. You don't master it. You apprentice yourself to it again and again. You let it teach you how to stay soft in the face of rejection, how to stay open in the presence of loss, how to stay rooted in the wildest unknown.

Eventually, the question stops being "Will I be chosen?" and becomes "Will I remain in integrity with myself, even when I am alone?" That is the ultimate sovereignty: the refusal to abandon yourself in the name of love. Because real love doesn't require that. It never did. What passes for love in its absence—compliance, performance, possession—is only a dim echo. But once you've heard the real sound, you can't return to the silence of suppression. You become fluent in a language that few people speak but everyone remembers in their bones.

You begin to recognize each other, those who live this way—not by their titles or beliefs, but by their resonance. The way their presence feels like home and horizon at once. The way their eyes carry the grief of letting go and the fire of what they've chosen instead. They don't need to prove anything. They're not recruiting. They are simply being. And in their being, you feel the possibilities of your own becoming. This is the secret economy of sovereign love: not extraction, but transmission; not consumption, but co creation.

In this new economy, the currency is coherence. The wealth is wisdom. The product is presence. And the metric is grace—not grace as politeness, but grace as power without coercion, the quiet might of someone who has nothing to prove and nothing to defend.

Someone who can walk away from the table without bitterness and walk toward themselves without delay. That kind of love builds things that last—not because they are rigid, but because they are alive, flexible, honest, fluid enough to adapt, anchored enough to endure.

To love as a sovereign is not to love without pain. It is to love with awareness, with boundaries, with devotion that is chosen, not extracted. It is to love with your eyes open, your heart unarmored, and your spirit unbribed. It is to bring the full force of your originality into every interaction, knowing it might not be met, and still offering it anyway—not to be accepted, but to be true. Because when you love like that, you change the room. Maybe not visibly. Maybe not instantly. But something shifts. Something loosens. Something remembers.

And even when you doubt yourself, even when your path seems invisible to others, sovereign love holds you—not like an external god, but like an inner gravity, the way the tide returns to the moon, the way your own name still sounds like music when spoken by someone who sees you. That gravity doesn't demand belief. It simply pulls you toward what matters. It pulls you toward the next honest word, the next bold step, the next wild truth that doesn't ask for permission. You don't need permission. You are the permission. You are the opening. You are the gate.

After Franklin Roosevelt's death, Eleanor Roosevelt could have retreated into widowhood's expected silence. Instead, sovereign love for human dignity pulled her toward her most important work. When Truman appointed her to chair the UN Human Rights Commission, diplomats dismissed her as "just a president's widow." She had no legal training, no diplomatic credentials. But her love for justice was sovereign—it needed no permission. Working eighteen hour days, she navigated between communist and capitalist ideologies, finding common ground in shared humanity. When the Declaration passed in 1948, she called it "the Magna Carta for all mankind." Her refusal to be diminished by others' expectations became the foundation for global human rights, proving that sovereign love creates its own authority.

And this is the disruptive grace of sovereign love: it creates its own reality—not as fantasy, but as fidelity, fidelity to what is real, even when it costs everything you once thought you needed, fidelity to your own design, your own depth, your own way of seeing. And from that fidelity, a new world emerges. Not all at once, not everywhere, but undeniably—through conversations, through invitations, through refusals that make room for yes, through the quiet building of a life that cannot be duplicated, only lived.

By the 1990s, Cash was considered a relic, his career seemingly over. Country music had moved past him; rock ignored him. He could have faded gracefully into retirement. Instead, sovereign love for authentic expression led him to producer Rick Rubin's garage studio. There, stripped of orchestration and artifice, Cash recorded covers of contemporary songs—Nine Inch Nails, Soundgarden, Depeche Mode—making them entirely his own. His voice, weathered by decades of living, transformed "Hurt" into a meditation on mortality that moved millions. He didn't chase relevance; he embodied it through radical honesty about aging, addiction, and redemption. Those final albums proved that sovereign love doesn't fade with time—it deepens, becoming more powerful as it sheds everything inauthentic.

In the end, sovereign love doesn't want your performance. It wants your presence, not your best self, your real self—the one who remembers that love is not something we fall into; it is something we become. And in becoming it, we set others free—not by saving them, but by showing them they were never trapped.

This is the invitation. This is the path. This is the promise.

You are not here to be chosen.

You are here to choose.

You are not here to fit in.

You are here to originate.

You are not here to earn love.

You are here to become it.

You've journeyed through the primal spark, the conscious gaze, the sacred vow, the sovereign act. Now you return not to the beginning, but to a higher version of it—equipped to love in motion, in system, in ritual, in vision. You return not to theory, but to life.

And once you do, the world will never be the same.

Sovereign Love

VISITATION
Love arrives uninvited as autonomous force.
Not possessed by us, but using us for its own mission.

DISRUPTION
Clears debris of false securities and control.
Creates clearing where only authenticity makes sense.

TRANSPARENCY
Becoming instrument of will greater than ego.
Fidelity to truth, not convention or consistency.

HONESTY
Living from essence rather than image.
Refusing to pretend for safety or acceptance.

COHERENCE
Inner and outer worlds stop contradicting.
Alignment becomes compass, truth becomes proof.

CREATION
Building new realities from sovereign frequency.
Generative force that invents rather than imitates.

TRANSMISSION
Permission for others to remember their sovereignty.
Showing they were never trapped.

Praxis Love: Reclaiming Human Presence

In this final chapter, we arrive at the realization that love—when practiced across time, scale, and structure—becomes regenerative. It doesn't just heal a wound or soothe an ache. It creates conditions where healing is the default, where connection, resilience, and meaning replicate themselves naturally, even across damaged landscapes—personal, political, or planetary.

To get here, we must revisit every kind of love we've explored and ask one final question: What happens when love becomes design? What happens when we build lives, communities, businesses, and governance around it—not as a feeling but as a framework for regeneration?

This is not utopian. It is ecological. Because in nature, love looks like reciprocity. In ecosystems, regeneration is not a miracle—it's the baseline. We're not writing a fairytale ending. We're planting seeds.

Love is not a static idea confined to pages or fleeting moments of tenderness. It is an active, embodied practice—a daily revolution that transforms the ordinary into the extraordinary. If you have journeyed through the map of love's theory—through its roots in survival, awareness, systems thinking, dreams, and devotion—you now stand at the threshold of its most vital truth: love is something you do.

In this chapter, we shift from understanding to action. Love as praxis means weaving love into every facet of your life—your relationships, your work, your self talk—and recognizing that this constant circulation creates a regenerative cycle. Like any economy worth its name, love requires exchange; it demands participation and maintenance for growth to flourish.

There comes a moment when love can no longer remain an idea. When all the dreaming, feeling, defining, and promising must give way to something else: enactment. Praxis. A way of moving through the world that makes love tangible—not as a gesture or a grand performance, but as method. Praxis Love is what happens when love matures beyond metaphor and enters muscle. It becomes the choreography of care, the discipline of daily compassion, the structure through which all other loves begin to breathe.

This love is not loud, and it is not romantic in the cinematic sense. It will not sweep you off your feet. Instead, it places your feet on the ground. It teaches you to stay. To return. To do again and again what might not yield immediate reward, but which, over time, alters reality. It is the kind of love that repairs rather than seduces, that builds systems rather than impressions, that writes policies, changes diapers, teaches without fanfare, and listens without waiting to respond.

To live in Praxis Love is to refuse the temptation of abstraction. It is to remember that love is only ever real when it becomes repeatable, when it shows up in action: in the way you structure your calendar, in the tone of your emails, in the architecture of your business, in the friction of contradiction. It demands embodiment. It demands that you become what you believe.

And this embodiment is not just personal—it is systemic. It is not enough to say that you love justice, or healing, or liberation. Praxis Love asks: Where does it show? In your hiring process? In your parenting? In your contracts? In your art? In how you end relationships? In how you treat your own body when no one is watching?

Praxis Love is love as logistics. Love as the inconvenient choice. Love as feedback integration. Love as patience in committee meetings. It is what the mystics were whispering about when they spoke of surrender—not the surrender of selfhood, but the surrender of illusion. The surrender of comfort. The surrender of the idea that love is a feeling rather than a daily construction.

The paradox is that Praxis Love can look, from the outside, ordinary. It will not always be visible. It often requires less speaking and more systems, fewer declarations and more consistency. You may not even be thanked. But that is the point. Praxis Love is devotional, not performative. It is love that chooses to stay in alignment with its values whether or not anyone else is watching.

It builds altars out of agendas. It sanctifies schedules. It turns meetings into rituals and habits into prayers. Not because it spiritualizes the mundane, but because it sees the sacred in the mundane. It knows that the way you send an invoice, the way you host a guest, the way you apologize—these are not details. These are design decisions. These are data points in the lived curriculum of love.

In this stage, love begins to code, to scaffold, to organize itself through people, processes, prototypes. You become a practitioner of love in the way an architect becomes a practitioner of space. You make love legible. Testable. Not to reduce it, but to incarnate it. This is where philosophy meets operations, where ethics meet execution, where the soul meets the spreadsheet.

And that is not a diminishment. It is an elevation. For what could be more sacred than the decision to bring grace into your infrastructure, to make fairness habitual, to code compassion into your UX, into your leadership styles, into your compensation frameworks? Love becomes a verb, yes—but more than that, it becomes system design.

Praxis Love is also iterative. It expects failure. It accommodates friction. It is not afraid of the messiness of reality because it understands love not as a perfect plan but as a living prototype. It is not brittle. It flexes. It listens to feedback. It adapts. Not because it is indecisive, but because it is alive. It evolves, the way ecosystems evolve—not by dominating, but by harmonizing.

So many relationships die not because love is gone, but because it never matured into praxis. It remained a wish, a mood, a high, a metaphor. But Praxis Love doesn't need a mood to function. It needs intention, attention, repetition. It understands that the most world changing forms of love may never feel like epiphany. They may feel like washing dishes, making edits, showing up on time, changing your mind.

In the grand arc of the twelve loves, Praxis is the culmination because it is the one that survives contact with reality. It is the love that doesn't vanish under pressure, but reorganizes pressure into alignment. It doesn't promise an escape. It promises a path—a path that is walked, not dreamed. A love you can live in. A love you can offer without fear of running out, because you've built the practices to replenish it.

Praxis Love is regenerative—not in theory, but in function. Not because it claims to save the world, but because it helps you design your corner of it sustainably, ethically, beautifully. It gives you something to do with your love. And in a world as fragile, fast, and hurting as ours, that might be the most revolutionary thing of all.

Imagine for a moment a circular economy—a system where resources are continually regenerated rather than exhausted. In such a system, what we give with love doesn't diminish us; it replenishes and revitalizes everything around us. When you choose kindness over indifference or patience over frustration, you contribute to this regenerative process. Every act of compassion is part of an ongoing flow that nurtures both giver and receiver.

There is no straight line through the twelve loves. There is only a spiral—expanding, deepening, returning. A choreography of movement where each love feeds the others, where each phase is both destination and departure point. And once you have walked them all, not once but again and again, you begin to understand that these loves are not stages. They are elements, instruments in a symphony, petals on a rotating flower.

Ignition Love begins it all—raw, primal, necessary. The fire that says I need you, I'm curious, I'm here. But without Conscious Love, that fire is wild and wasteful. Awareness tames it. Attention shapes it. Presence anchors it in now. Still, love cannot live on perception alone—it needs Worthy Love to take a stand, to declare I matter— and so do you. Identity is not narcissism—it is the root of discernment.

But selfhood is not enough. To endure, love must scale—enter Systemic Love. The love of structure, of equity, of invisible scaffolding that lets care survive the weight of time. And structure alone can calcify unless it breathes. That's when Relational Love flows in—the water between the stones, the dance of empathy and reciprocity. You learn that no structure matters unless it holds us, not just me.

And then the current shifts again: love needs to move, not just stay. Tradeable Love reminds you that circulation is survival, that withheld love starves everyone. But flow without vision is just motion. Enter Visionary Love. The boldness to imagine, to ask What if? What if we dared to love not just what is, but what could be?

Once that dream is born, Devotional Love picks up the thread. It repeats the dream. It polishes it. Turns it into rhythm, into incense, into promise. And from that promise, Radiant Love glows—not forced, not posed, just true. The kind of love that does not broadcast—it simply transmits. The kind of love that feels like sunlight.

But even sunlight needs a structure to refract through, a window, a prism. That's when Fractal Love arrives—showing you how the small mirrors the vast, how a single act moves across networks, how a soft word to a child becomes a policy twenty years later. You begin to live at all scales at once. You zoom out. You zoom in. You stop pretending anything is isolated.

And then, just when you think you've reached transcendence, Covenantal Love grounds you again, reminding you that dreams need contracts, that magic becomes real when people agree, that futures are built not just on feelings but on shared vows—the kind that aren't just said, but lived, rewritten, respected, not out of obligation but out of alignment.

Then finally—Sovereign Love. The hardest one to teach, because it cannot be given. It must be claimed. It is the moment love becomes not just a practice or a gift, but a force—your force, the way you shape time and space, the way you rewrite the rules without needing permission, the love that moves not because it is invited, but because it is inevitable.

And yet even Sovereign Love cannot stand alone. It circles back to Praxis. Praxis is the house that holds them all, the cathedral made of every moment, every gesture, every contradiction woven back into coherence. Praxis is what love becomes when all its forms are practiced, not just praised. When love is no longer a search, but a stance. No longer a question, but a craft.

This is the spiral. Not ascending into perfection, but deepening into integrity. Not escaping the world, but embodying it differently. Letting love show up through systems, through bodies, through businesses, through poems, through logistics, through silence, through spreadsheets, through cities.

You begin to see that love was never the what. It was the how— the way you wrote the email, the way you ended the meeting, the way you held your child, the way you listened when it would have been easier to argue, the way you fired someone with dignity, the way you forgave yourself for not knowing sooner, the way you said no, the way you said yes again.

To walk the twelve loves is to become a steward of something bigger than yourself. It is to remember that love is not a trait you have, or a mood you wait for, or a feeling you chase. It is a method, a responsibility, a technology, a ritual, a risk, a refuge, a revolution.

And more than anything else, it is work—not the kind of work that burns you out, but the kind of work that builds you, the kind of work that makes your life feel like it matters—not because you were good, but because you were real, because you kept showing up, because your love was not perfect but it was practiced.

Praxis Love also challenges us to see our everyday routines as opportunities for revolution. Small acts—smiling at a stranger on the street, offering genuine appreciation to a colleague, choosing patience instead of anger in moments of conflict—these are not trivialities but foundational acts that uphold the larger structure of compassionate living. These acts are quiet architecture—they shape the emotional infrastructure of the world we inhabit.

In 2019, the Business Roundtable—an association of CEOs from America's largest corporations—did something unprecedented. They abandoned shareholder primacy, the doctrine that had governed corporate America for nearly fifty years, and embraced stakeholder capitalism. In a single statement, they declared that businesses should serve not just shareholders, but customers, employees, suppliers, communities, and the environment.

This wasn't sentiment. This was systems thinking. This was love becoming economic theory.

For decades, the dominant model of capitalism operated on a simple premise: maximize shareholder value, and the invisible hand of the market will optimize everything else. It was elegant in its simplicity and brutal in its application. Companies that prioritized anything other than profit were considered inefficient, even irresponsible to their investors.

But something shifted. Perhaps it was the mounting evidence that short-term profit maximization was destroying the very ecosystems—environmental, social, economic—that business depends on. Perhaps it was the recognition that companies treating workers, communities, and the planet as externalities were ultimately undermining their own sustainability. Or perhaps it was the growing understanding that in a hyperconnected world, there is no such thing as a purely isolated transaction.

Whatever the catalyst, we are witnessing the emergence of economic models that look remarkably like love made manifest. Not the romantic fantasy of love, but love as we've been exploring it throughout this journey—love as intelligent design for regenerative systems.

Kate Raworth's Doughnut Economics provides perhaps the clearest example of how love principles are being embedded into economic theory. The doughnut model suggests that a healthy economy operates within two boundaries: a social foundation that ensures everyone has access to life's essentials (housing, healthcare, education, democratic participation) and an ecological ceiling that ensures we don't overshoot planetary or community boundaries.

It's the recognition that true prosperity requires designing systems that work for everyone, not just the winners of competitive markets. It's the understanding that we are in a covenant with future generations and with the planet itself.

Cities like Amsterdam, Copenhagen, and Portland have begun implementing doughnut economics at the municipal level. They're not just measuring GDP growth; they're measuring wellbeing, sustainability, and social equity. They're designing policies that recognize the interconnectedness of human and ecological health.

This is what happens when love becomes municipal policy, when care becomes the organizing principle of governance, when the question shifts from "How do we maximize output?" to "How do we create conditions where all life can thrive?"

Anthropologist Marcel Mauss identified something profound about gift economies: they create stronger social bonds than market economies. When you give someone a gift, you create a relationship. When you sell someone something, you complete a transaction.

But this isn't just about business strategy. It's about recognizing that the most generative economic activities are those that strengthen social fabric rather than extract from it. It's about understanding that the circulation of care, attention, and resources creates abundance in ways that hoarding never could.

This is love as economic engine. Love as the foundation of innovation. Love as the source of genuine value creation.

Perhaps the most radical development in contemporary economic theory is the emergence of regenerative capitalism—the idea that business should leave the world better than it found it. This goes beyond sustainability (doing less harm) to regeneration (actively healing damaged systems).

This is Praxis Love at corporate scale. It's the recognition that in a world facing climate crisis, social inequality, and political instability, businesses that focus solely on extraction and growth are not just morally questionable—they're strategically obsolete.

Regenerative capitalism understands that in complex systems, the health of the whole determines the health of the parts. Companies that invest in the health of their communities, their ecosystems, and their employees don't just do good—they perform better over the long term.

Childcare, eldercare, community building, emotional labor, household management, volunteering—this work is essential to human flourishing but invisible to GDP calculations. Some countries are beginning to measure and value this work. New Zealand includes unpaid work in its national accounts. Bhutan measures Gross National Happiness rather than just Gross Domestic Product.

These stories are not mere anecdotes; they are beacons illuminating a future where capitalism becomes a vessel for love's transformative power. They reveal that when we design with empathy, act with compassion, and build systems rooted in care, we forge economies capable of regenerating life itself. Love, in this context, is not passive sentiment but an active, relentless force—an ethic that guides us through systemic barriers and cultural norms toward a horizon where prosperity is measured by the health of ecosystems, the resilience of communities, and the dignity of every life.

It's the recognition that what we pay attention to shapes what we value, and what we value shapes what we create. When we make care work visible and valuable, we create economic systems that support human flourishing rather than just material accumulation.

This shift from extraction to regeneration is not just an economic revolution—it's a love revolution. It's the recognition that Praxis Love requires us to design systems that serve life rather than deplete it. It requires us to become stewards of the systems we're part of rather than just beneficiaries of them.

These acts are quiet architecture—they shape the emotional infrastructure of the world we inhabit.

This love doesn't need to be understood to be trusted. It only asks that you begin, that you build, that you dare to live your values out loud—in form, in action, in contradiction; that you let your love grow limbs, take shape, bear weight.

Remember that this love isn't just about personal fulfillment; it's revolutionary because it redefines how societies operate at their core—from economic models grounded solely in profit toward those rooted equally in wellbeing and shared prosperity, what some now call "regenerative capitalism." In such economies, giving back isn't charity—it's essential investment into collective health.

And in doing so, you become the architecture of everything you once prayed for. You become the builder of a new world.

As we stand at this crossroads, the question is not whether love can reshape capitalism but whether we have the courage to let it. The answer lies in our willingness to reimagine, to listen deeply, and to act boldly. Because in the end, love is the most potent design principle of all—an enduring blueprint for a future where economies serve life, not just markets. The choice is ours: to continue building walls or to dismantle them with care, to forge systems that heal rather than harm, and to embrace love as the guiding force toward a truly regenerative future.

So here lies your invitation:

To practice Praxis Love—daily, imperfectly, intentionally.

To become an architect of love—building it into systems, embedding it in structures, making it inevitable rather than accidental.

Start where you are. Use what you have. Design what matters.

In your morning routine. In your hiring process. In how you structure meetings. In the way you apologize. In your pricing model. In your parenting. In your governance. In your grief.

Because love is not a feeling waiting to be felt.

It is infrastructure waiting to be built.

Build it, brick by brick, choice by choice, system by system.

Until love becomes the default setting.

Until compassion becomes the operating principle.

Until regeneration becomes the baseline.

This is not the end of theory. It is the beginning of practice.

Not the conclusion of philosophy, but the commencement of engineering.

Love as the design for everything we build next.

Love as the technology that transforms worlds.

Love as the only architecture strong enough to hold our future.

Praxis Love

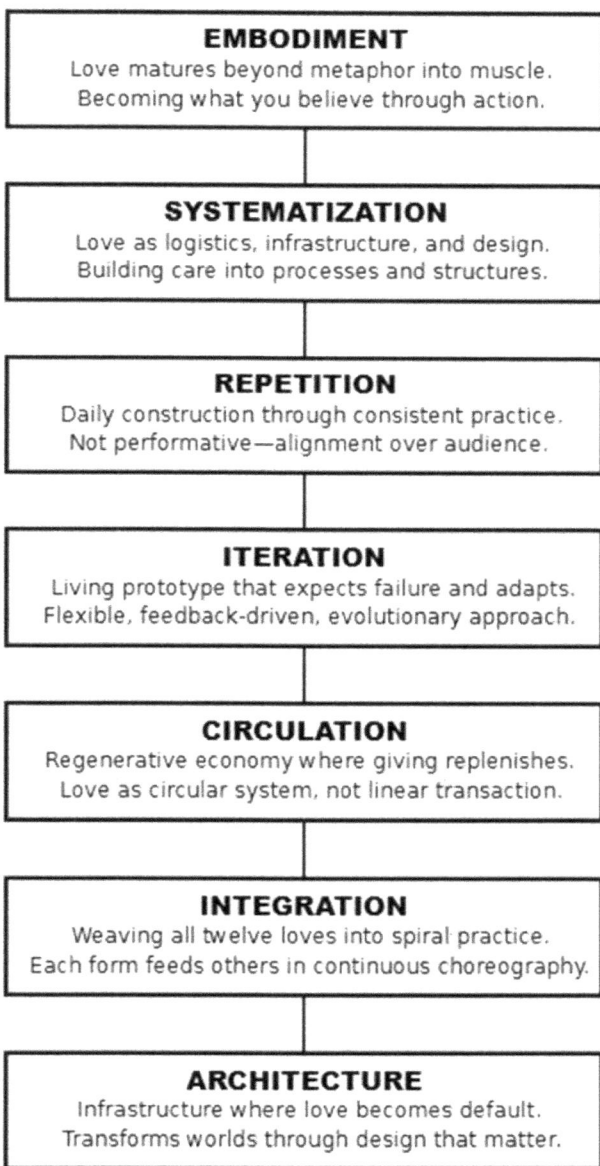

EMBODIMENT
Love matures beyond metaphor into muscle.
Becoming what you believe through action.

SYSTEMATIZATION
Love as logistics, infrastructure, and design.
Building care into processes and structures.

REPETITION
Daily construction through consistent practice.
Not performative—alignment over audience.

ITERATION
Living prototype that expects failure and adapts.
Flexible, feedback-driven, evolutionary approach.

CIRCULATION
Regenerative economy where giving replenishes.
Love as circular system, not linear transaction.

INTEGRATION
Weaving all twelve loves into spiral practice.
Each form feeds others in continuous choreography.

ARCHITECTURE
Infrastructure where love becomes default.
Transforms worlds through design that matter.

From Poetic to Practical: Accessing Love's Principles

As we journey through the ideas in this book, the true power lies in moving from theory to practice—bringing love's principles alive in everyday life, work, and leadership. This chapter offers a practical toolkit to help you do exactly that: tools that are accessible, adaptable, and deeply transformative.

At the heart of this toolkit are reflection prompts—simple yet profound questions designed to ignite awareness and spark change. Awareness is the soil where love takes root; without it, love remains an abstract ideal. Through reflection, you begin to notice where love flows freely and where it is blocked or distorted. You start to see how your presence, your boundaries, your systems, and your legacy are shaped—sometimes unconsciously—by forces that may or may not align with love's essence. Let's begin with a foundational exercise: a Presence Audit.

Presence Audit: Where Do You Truly Show Up?

Presence is often spoken of as a spiritual or emotional ideal, but it's also a practical skill—the ability to be fully attentive and engaged with what's happening here and now. In leadership and organizational life, presence transforms routine interactions into moments of connection, understanding, and empowerment.

Reflect on this:

• Where in your life or organization do you show up fully?

• Where do you find yourself "going through the motions," disconnected or distracted?

• What changes when you commit to giving full attention in these moments?

Many of us carry habits of half presence, fueled by busyness, distraction, or the pressure to perform. We attend meetings while mentally multitasking, listen to others but plan our response instead of truly hearing, or engage in rituals that no longer serve their original purpose. This fragmented presence creates dissonance—it weakens trust, stifles creativity, and erodes the relational fabric that holds groups together.

But when you consciously choose to be present, even in small moments, you make a powerful declaration: "I see you. This matters. We matter." This simple act—focused attention—becomes an act of love. It builds relational capital, the invisible but essential currency of trust and belonging.

Practical Tip: Begin by picking one daily activity—a team meeting, a one-on-one conversation, or even your morning routine. Before you start, take three mindful breaths. Notice your body, your emotions, your thoughts. Commit to being fully present for the duration. Observe what shifts in the energy and outcomes.

Worthy Boundaries: Holding Values with Love

Boundaries often carry a negative connotation—seen as barriers or limitations. Yet, in the context of love, boundaries are the sacred edges that protect our integrity and capacity to give fully. Without boundaries, love becomes a depleting resource, stretched thin and losing its vitality.

Ask yourself:

• What values or boundaries do you silently compromise in the name of harmony or success?

• How might it feel to hold those boundaries firmly—and lovingly?

In organizations, boundary compromises often masquerade as flexibility or teamwork but can lead to burnout, resentment, and erosion of core principles. For example, leaders who avoid difficult conversations to keep peace may unintentionally undermine trust and authenticity. Employees who overwork to please may sacrifice health and creativity.

Love based leadership invites us to rethink boundaries not as walls but as guardians of mutual respect and sustainable connection. Setting boundaries with love means clearly

communicating your needs and limits while honoring others'
needs. It is an act of courage and compassion.

Practical Tip: Identify one boundary you have been hesitant to
assert—perhaps around work hours, communication styles, or
decision-making authority. Write down what that boundary looks
like and why it matters to your wellbeing or your team's health.
Plan how you can express this boundary clearly and kindly in the
coming week.

Systemic Honesty: Evaluating Structures Through a Lens of Care

Love is not just an interpersonal phenomenon; it also manifests in the systems and structures we create. Policies, processes, roles, and rituals reflect the values we embody—whether consciously or by default.

Consider:

• Which of your current structures reflect genuine care and nurturing?

• Which exist primarily out of convenience, legacy, or fear?

Systems that reflect love prioritize dignity, growth, and connection. They create safety, enable recognition, foster belonging, and invite truth telling. Conversely, systems built around convenience or fear may enforce compliance, limit voice, and perpetuate inequities.

This reflection invites courageous honesty. It's tempting to defend existing structures as necessary or efficient, but love asks us to be curious and vulnerable: Are these structures serving the whole or just maintaining the status quo? Are they nurturing or extracting?

Practical Tip: Choose one system or process in your organization—such as hiring, feedback, or conflict resolution. Map it out and evaluate it through the lens of care. Identify one change you can make to increase its alignment with love based principles.

Building on the reflective foundation, this section shifts toward design practices—concrete ways to translate insights into systemic change. Reflection awakens awareness; design shapes that awareness into structures that embody love's principles. These practices serve as practical guides to intentionally craft environments where safety, recognition, belonging, clear boundaries, and truth can flourish.

Praxis Love Mapping: Designing with Heart, then Logic

One of the most effective ways to bring love into systems is through "Praxis Love" Mapping—a practice of taking any existing organizational process and redesigning it explicitly with love at the center.

Start by choosing one process or area—examples might include:

- Onboarding new team members

- Running meetings

- Performance reviews

- Customer service protocols

Ask:

What would this look like if it were designed with love, not just logic?

Logical design often focuses on efficiency, compliance, or risk avoidance. A love-centered design expands the focus to include emotional safety, human dignity, and meaningful connection.

For example, onboarding might shift from a checklist-driven exercise to a ritual of welcome that includes:

- Personal introductions and storytelling to build belonging

- Clear, loving communication about expectations and boundaries

- Opportunities for new hires to express their hopes and concerns

- Space for mentors to offer recognition and support

By mapping the current state against this vision, you can identify gaps—moments where care is missing or where the process feels mechanical. Then redesign with intentional focus on these five pillars:

1. **Safety**: Does the process create psychological and emotional safety?

2. **Recognition**: Are individuals genuinely seen and valued?

3. **Belonging**: Does it foster a sense of connection and shared purpose?

4. **Clear Boundaries**: Are expectations and limits communicated with respect?

5. **Space for Truth**: Is there room for honest dialogue without fear?

This mapping can reveal surprising opportunities for small changes with outsized impact. It's a creative and compassionate approach that turns systems from cold mechanisms into living relationships.

Practical Tip: After redesigning, pilot your new process with a small group. Invite honest feedback focused not just on what worked functionally but on how people felt held or seen. Use this feedback to iterate.

Values Into Infrastructure: Embedding Love in Everyday Systems

Many organizations claim inspiring values—transparency, dignity, curiosity—but these values often remain aspirational, disconnected from day to day reality. Translating values into infrastructure means making those principles visible, tangible, and actionable in your systems and routines.

Begin by listing the core values you or your team cherish. For example:

- Curiosity

- Transparency

- Dignity

- Compassion

Then ask:

- Where are these values currently visible in our processes, communication, and policies?

- Where are they absent or even contradicted?

- How might we redesign or create infrastructure that amplifies these values?

For instance, if transparency is a core value but performance feedback is sporadic or opaque, consider creating regular, structured feedback loops where peers and leaders share observations with kindness and clarity. If dignity is central, review your language and communication channels for anything that feels dismissive or punitive—and redesign accordingly.

This practice brings values off the wall and into lived experience, reinforcing alignment between what you say and how you act.

Practical Tip: Create a values infrastructure "audit" with your team quarterly. Review one or two core values and collaboratively assess how well current systems uphold them. Brainstorm practical shifts and commit to one concrete change.

Misunderstanding Risk Plan: Preparing to Hold Space Under Pressure

Systems and behaviors rooted in love are deeply powerful but can also be vulnerable to misunderstanding. Acts of care or boundary setting may be misread as weakness, indecisiveness, or exclusion—especially in environments accustomed to competition, hierarchy, or rapid results.

A **Misunderstanding Risk Plan** prepares you and your organization to anticipate, name, and respond to such misinterpretations with clarity and strength.

Ask:

• Where might our care be misread as weakness or lack of rigor?

• How do we explain and defend our values and practices under pressure or criticism?

• Who in our team is responsible for holding this language and modeling these responses?

For example, a love-based policy encouraging flexible work schedules may be challenged as "lax" by those focused solely on output. A Misunderstanding Risk Plan might include clear data on productivity, stories of improved well being, and a communication script that reaffirms the commitment to excellence through care.

By preparing this plan, you create a safe container where love-centered innovation can thrive without being derailed by fear or misunderstanding.

Practical Tip: Roleplay challenging conversations where love based values might be questioned. Practice responding with calm, grounded language that invites curiosity rather than defensiveness. Document and share these responses as part of organizational learning.

Feedback Circles of Love: Compassionate Listening

Feedback is often seen narrowly as performance evaluation. Love expands feedback into a tool for relational health and systemic evolution.

Feedback Circles of Love are intentionally designed spaces where people share not just how well tasks are done but how well the system holds them—emotionally, psychologically, and practically.

Facilitate these circles with questions like:

- Where do you feel most supported and held by this system?

- Where do you feel unseen, unheard, or expendable?

- What small changes could help this system better nurture you and others?

The key is to create non judgmental, brave spaces where feedback is not punishment but invitation—an invitation to grow, deepen connection, and realign structures with shared values.

Regular feedback cycles help organizations stay attuned to the lived experience of their members, identifying emerging issues before they escalate and celebrating what's working well.

Practical Tip: Start with a small, trusted team and hold monthly feedback circles. Use anonymous tools if needed to create safety. Ensure leadership participates authentically and acts visibly on the feedback.

Integrating Design Practices: From Intention to Impact

Each of these design practices—Praxis Love Mapping, Values Into Infrastructure, Misunderstanding Risk Planning, and Feedback Circles of Love—functions as a node in a living ecosystem. Together, they enable continuous reflection, intentional design, resilience under pressure, and relational evolution.

To embed them sustainably:

• Schedule regular reflection and design workshops where teams revisit these questions and practices.

• Document insights and decisions transparently to create shared memory and accountability.

• Celebrate progress and openly explore challenges as part of the growth process.

This toolkit is not a one time fix but an ongoing commitment to bringing love's principles into the messy, complex reality of human organizations. It invites courage, patience, and generosity—but the rewards are profound: environments where people thrive, creativity blossoms, and collective impact deepens.